Sunfl...
my Table

War Diaries
of a Ukrainian
Community

Amber Poole

WHITE CROW

www.whitecrowbooks.com

Sunflowers at my Table

Copyright © 2024 by Amber Poole. All rights reserved.

Published by White Crow Books, an imprint
of White Crow Productions Ltd.

The right of Amber Poole to be identified as the author
of this work has been asserted by her in accordance
with the Copyright, Design and Patents act 1988.

A CIP catalogue record for this book is
available from the British Library.

For information, contact White Crow Books by
e-mail: info@whitecrowbooks.com.

Cover Design by Astrid@Astridpaints.com
Cover Image by Andrei Pechenizkyi
Interior design by Velin@Perseus-Design.com

Paperback: ISBN: 978-1-78677-262-6
eBook: ISBN: 978-1-78677-263-3

NON-FICTION / Diaries & Journals / War

www.whitecrowbooks.com

Sunflowers at my Table

Contents

Acknowledgments

~

Of the many people who contributed to the story told in these War Diaries, a special thanks goes to Basia Rostworowska, who read aloud each diary entry on Morley Radio, the community radio station for Morley College, London.

We could not have run our household without the help of our tireless staff, Dorota Wyraz, Małgorzata 'Gosia' Lech, and Agnieszka Wawryk.

A big thanks also to Ruedi Mauch, Bożena Sarniak and Ewa Kuczyńska, who translated several entries into German and in Polish, to circulate our story to a wider audience.

Great thanks to our sponsors, without whose help, The Cross Border House would have never survived for as long as it did.

We also thank our Ukrainian community, for sharing their stories, their hopes, sorrows, and for supporting us when we needed them.

Thank you, Jonathan Beecher, for considering our work important enough to publish.

Amber & Paul

Prologue

~

We were sitting around a table at the Kurozwęki mini brew, drinking champagne and eating sushi. For Amber and I, it was meant to be a carefree celebration where we could forget our personal cares and the world. However we were both acutely aware of the rumours of war. Russian troop movements across the Ukrainian border, but three hours drive from us, were in the news. All the experts gave reasons why there would be no war – that it was foolishness, it could not be won, what would be the point and so on.

Andrew Popiel and Agnieszka Szataniak so wanted to celebrate Valentine's Day with us that they arranged for a driver to pick us up and drive us from Sichów to Kurozwęki. Sichów was our home, an eighteenth-century manor home, once the residence of the Potocki and Radziwiłł family, now owned by our cousin Stefan

Dunin-Wąsowicz, who also joined us that evening. For six years we had run an educational centre there. We organised meditation groups, art workshops, music events and children's events. The house could accommodate forty guests, but it was now standing empty, except for Amber and I. No one travelled much during the winter months, and we did not anticipate any guests until at least April.

Despite the experts, Amber and I expected that war would break out. In this we were guided mainly by our dreams. We are both students of C.G. Jung's depth psychology, and our experience has shown that dreams can provide valuable guidance and are not to be ignored. A little like an internal early warning signal. For several months, both of us had had dreams of war. There were falling bombs, troop movements and so on. Amber once dreamed of many bombs falling around Sichów, but in a later scene, realised that they were all falling on the other side of a fence. We ourselves were safe.

If war broke out in the Ukraine, how would we experience it? According to Amber's dream, we ourselves would be safe, something I was sure of regardless of other considerations. However there would be refugees fleeing across the border to Poland.

"They'll be coming by the busload," I said to the group sitting with me. "What do you think we'll do when the first busload of refugees stops by our house?"

Why should they stop by our house? Because we are equipped to host such a group – professional kitchen, rooms, beds – everything they would need to stay safe and wait out the war.

I'm not sure who answered my question, Amber, myself or someone else at the table, but the answer was obvious at any rate.

"We open our doors."

None of us asked why we should do it. For myself, there was no thought of social duty, altruism, idealism, Christian charity or any of that. I had never been a social activist, actually I had actively avoided being one. We didn't think about who would pay for it, or what personal cost there would be. Nor did we think of later consequences, such as cancelling our summer educational programme.

This was just something that we had to do.

The idea of turning Sichów into a home for families fleeing the destruction of war did not however come out of the blue. It was part of my family history, stories that we often related to others, stories that we referenced. Eighty years earlier, my mother Rose Kieniewicz, living in Ruszcza, a manor home outside of Kraków, was sleeping on a couch in the corridor, as all available beds were taken up by war refugees. This was the time of the German occupation of Poland during World War II. Rose was only twenty years old when the war broke out. She had married three months earlier, barely had moved into her home when her husband left to join his regiment. Later he was captured and spent the following five years in a POW camp. Rose had to manage the household and the farm. There were fields of cereal, gardens and farm animals. She had competent estate managers and so mainly occupied herself with affairs of the house. Fortunately, during the following years the farm produced enough food to support the household at a time when nothing else was working.

And then there were the refugees. The war had destroyed many homes in Warsaw and other cities. Families were looking for shelter, some were close aunts or cousins related to Rose, but many were just friends of friends who had lost their homes. Later on there came Jews who were being hunted. One report we heard was of a blind Jewish man that Rose took in at considerable risk to herself and her home.

Rose kept an abbreviated diary of her daily activities, that in all ran to no more than 20 pages. Much of this diary reflected her inner life. At a time when the outer world was falling apart, and one could not see anything encouraging outside, it was her inner life that provided strength and stability.

From her diary:

A. Organization. Get up early. Indicate what work needs to be done. The cleaning, all corners of the house.

B. Dedicate a specific hour in which everything in the larder is passed out. Give money to those who need it.

C. Let all know the day before what duties will need doing the day after.

D. Don't put out so much sugar when serving tea. Think about everything you do beforehand. Careful not to waste food.

E. Take care of the furniture and be sure it doesn't fall into disrepair. The things that are broken, put in another place so they can be mended.

F. Clean windows, beat rugs, wash linen, pack winter coats in moth balls, polish the door handles. Put everything on the calendar.

G. Consider the relationships of the poor and the other house guests, take to heart their destiny. Don't ask ordinary questions. Ask myself if I have done everything for them. Look for Jesus in them and believe that Jesus is in me and will do something through me. Listen to them with great attention. Try to console them. Don't say superficial things to them but with the real love which you have within you, enter into work alongside them and make an effort to make it easier.

Two years later Rose herself was a refugee. She escaped Communist Poland and met up with her husband in Germany. The war had taken away their homes, their land, everything familiar. For my father, it was the third time he had lost his home. The Russian revolution destroyed the family home in eastern Poland. The home in Warsaw was bombed out. Then Ruszcza was confiscated by the Communist government. My parents ended up in Scotland, a land whose language they didn't speak, whose culture was unfamiliar. Growing up in Scotland, I was acutely aware of being in a foreign land. Of being different. Perhaps that was why the idea of hosting Ukrainian refugees at Sichów almost felt like the family business.

Did I have the strength to take care of the needs of forty refugees at Sichów? I didn't ask myself that question. Nor did I ask, where the money for such an undertaking would come from. For six years Amber and I ran an educational foundation, but it was of meagre means, especially during the winter when we had no income and had to pay high utility bills. However, our Constitution did say that we were dedicated to supporting national minorities, and Ukrainians were a national minority.

On February 24, war broke out, starting with a barrage of bombing of major Ukrainian cities. Troops were mobilized on both sides and the shooting began. Refugees began to stream into Poland, mostly women and children. Ukrainian men of military age were forbidden to leave the country. Very soon our friends began to call us asking whether we could take in some families they knew about. We said, "Yes," and waited. Meanwhile I posted on Facebook, that we were taking in Ukrainians, and needed donations to cover our expenses. The donations came in, a trickle that grew into a flood. Most of them came via my Facebook post from friends in the USA and the UK. I remember the feeling of amazement at seeing the donations come in. On Friday evenings I hosted an online forum for the Scientific and Medical Network, an educational charity based in the UK. Everyone was asking me about the refugees. They all wanted to know how they could help.

The first group arrived by car. They were probably more affluent than those who came after, but we never inquired after anyone's financial standing, regardless of the make of their car. The following groups were different. They came by chartered bus, some directly from the border, some from Kraków. I'd get a phone call from a woman who said, "I'm heading for Kraków to the refugee centre. How many families can you take?" The refugee centre was a fire station where families lay on floor mattresses and were fed sandwiches. Stomach flu and other diseases were rampant.

We could see the confusion in their eyes, looks of fear, distress. Some of them had seen terrible things. We showed them their rooms. They'd shut their doors. Often we didn't see them again for several days. We didn't screen them, ask who they were, or whether they had any criminal record. However, all of them only

16

expected to stay with us for a few months. They were convinced that the war wouldn't last longer.

After a few days Stefan left for Warsaw. He speaks Russian, and decided to volunteer at Warsaw railway station to speak to new arrivals. Refugees tended to head for the large cities where there was a better chance for work. One afternoon he saw a family of five waiting for a train. The father of two children was obviously quite ill. They were heading for Łódz, as hotels were reportedly cheaper there. They had spent some days in a sports stadium and the children had become sick. Stefan put them on a bus headed for Sichów. We met them that evening.

Today our centre is closed, families have now moved on to independent living. We were able to subsidise the relocation of many families thanks to a generous grant and donations. We ourselves now live in another part of Poland. Yet many families we lived with remain as part of our lives. We are in contact with many of them. For eighteen months we were a community, living together, creating art, theatre sharing our joys, suffering and quarrelling, but also celebrating each other's lives. No birthday passed uncelebrated.

The Diaries give a glimpse into this time. They are not only a prosaic account of events that took place but tell a larger story. What the time together feel for us and for our residents. What were their dreams, those shattered by war, other dreams of a new future? What world did they dream of for their children?

Paul Kieniewicz, Przychodzko,
Poland 2023

Introduction

"There is no one there, there is a mystery
And a simple, clear, terrible silence
Lights from the window on the floor
And everywhere the long shadows of the night
Like an unreasonable and ridiculous cry.
Understand: a locked apartment."

"... And here beyond the window, a sunflower is getting
Wet in the rain ..."

Grażyna Chrostowska, poet, activist of the Polish
Underground
Executed, Shot on April 18, 1942 (Age 22)
Ravensbruck

I fell in love. That's what happened. I simply fell in love with it all. Head over heels. I fell in love with the chaos, the stories, the children, their families, the imperfections and the irritations that go along with falling in love. I fell hard.

That's what I tell people who ask me endless questions about how was it possible to shelter so many for so long without giving up. The truth of the matter is, we sheltered each other.

The world has moved on from the start of the war. Few are interested anymore in the lives of the Ukrainian refugees, but there was a time when the mist lifted, much like in the disappearing town of Brigadoon, when the magic curse forgot about itself and we were there together, living, creating, grieving, fearing, imagining.

It was after ten in the evening when the first bus arrived carrying around fifteen, twenty people.

The first week in March we were still in the custody of winter. It was damp and cold and late. I remember so clearly when everyone started unloading with their shopping bags filled to capacity; in some cases, the contents spilling out onto the ground. If I tried to help by taking one, there was a noticeable resistance. These women clutched everything they carried, tightly, gripping each bag with all their might as if to say: Do not touch anything I have, do not come too close. Do not take anything else away from me. Sleepy children clung to the necks of their mothers. There were a few dogs and a cat, but more distinctly what I remember from that night is the look of disorientation, mistrust, disbelief, and fear in everyone's eyes. In the truest sense of the word, it was surreal.

One family, whom I later learned were the Pechenizkyi's, climbed out of the bus as a unit, as if threaded together by an invisible chord. Grandparents, daughters, granddaughters. Paul and I had already decided that the grandparents would sleep in a ground floor room while the daughters and granddaughters would accommodate another on the second floor. We assumed the seniors would want privacy but nothing could have been further from the truth. As Gala, their daughter, was following Paul to the upper floor, her mother cried out, "That's my daughter. Wait. Where is she going? Where are you taking her? That's my daughter." I'm quite certain that's when it happened, when I fell in love. I knew I was face to face with a sacred archetype; the story of woman – as mother – as daughter, trapped by war, on the run by force, without choice, without freedom. Never had I come so close to experiencing the collective vulnerability of woman in peril as I did upon hearing the call of a mother for her daughter.

Kate Burns writes in her book, *Paths to Transformation:* "Re-examining call, crisis, and cure, a few essential ideas bear repetition. Call announces a psychic drive toward renewal, that is, inner psychic enactment of the archetype of initiation, and may appear at any time in an individual's life."

At that moment, an inner fusion took place. A profoundly transformative psychic drive had risen up within me. Standing in place at the foot of the stair, all that was wrong in the world, and all that was right, crystallised in that split second of hearing a mother calling out for her daughter. Within that primordial, immaculate instant, that fissure between two sounds, where the authenticity of truth dwells, at that moment, upon hearing a daughter's name called out by her mother took hold of me with such love that I knew there could be no equivocating as to the question of whether or not it was our responsibility to create a home for these women, or whether we were even exercising good judgement to do so in the first place; that action, that commitment was not negotiable. I was one with these women, and for all the other people who proffered up their unwanted opinions about how Paul and I indulged them in our protective care by providing food too good for them, nice birthday parties, new shoes for the children, field trips and art classes, did nothing except to infuriate me. Especially those men and women from whom I least expected such contempt, this uncensored loathing, shameless attitude of hatred and racism which turned to exploitation before ones very eyes. How could those who were safe from the consequence of war, those who were living a good economic life demonstrate such insensitivity, not in the least those whose own ancestors had fled from war themselves not but one generation earlier?

It is true that no country is prepared to accept upward of two million people overnight, without a plan in place and no country that I know of has one. We are not educated to care for each other. Even within our own families, where intimacy should logically hold priority status, there is an irritation when one member of the tribe needs care. Sacrifice is an inconvenience, so I understand that to ask an entire country to re-design its infrastructure so as to care for a stranger is improbable and unfair considering the current cultural, social climate of identifying refugees as a threat.

After the shelter closed and the residents were re-established, and Paul and I moved to the north of Poland, I asked myself if these diaries were of any value to anyone. What is their relevance, if any? They served a great purpose while we all lived together; our very survival, in fact, depended on them. They were written and distributed on a regular basis to encourage the donations we required to provide adequate care. We were exceedingly fortunate to have received sizeable donations from so many around the world; our work wouldn't have been possible without each and every donor. My thanks is great.

Beyond the seventeen months we actually sheltered together, the grant monies and occasional donations the Foundation still receives are now used to pay for rent and food and medicine for the Ukrainians who still have no work.

I ask. What purpose do these diaries serve today, now that we have all gone our separate ways? It is at best a thoughtful question; one which I've examined in long consideration.

It is friendship that I hope for the reader. If, in discovering friendship with the residents from The Cross Border House there might be an action of heart which could then lead to an acknowledgment of the gravity of what it means to be a refugee from any country, then this would be my wish. The world is teeming with displaced, lonely people. Inescapable is their confinement. Their loss of home, their refugee status, those seeking asylum.

If these diaries awaken in the reader curiosity enough to even ask the most basic question of how another's homelessness affects us, then the publication of these entries has been worth it.

Every displaced person on the planet leaves behind a locked apartment.

Amber Poole Kieniewicz
September 25, 2023,
Przychodzko, Poland

WAR DIARY

Tuesday, March 8, 2022

My ex-husband called this morning to see if he could help by sending money and spreading the word in San Diego. He asked: "Tell me about a typical day."

What an interesting turn of phrase as there is no typical day. Getting coffee and starting a fire in the downstairs fireplace is where typical ends. But one does look forward to the coffee and the warmth of the fire, dare I say, we count on it in a world where counting on anything is a precarious business.

Twenty-eight refugees in your house quickly converts a person's thinking from the theoretical to the actual. No longer do I speak in the abstract. Every night as I climb into bed, I am struck by the visceral and the practical in each minute of my day.

I never knew one could contain so many emotions and complexes in one body, and then to multiply that by 28 is what the house and the land must support. And then remembering the Nazis that drove up the driveway in 1940 to take our family, Zofia and Krzystof to Ravensbruck and Majdanek respectively is the atmosphere at Sichów.

While there is no actual threat to Poland, the Poles and the Ukrainians share the same memories of an ancestral past which is still tangible, real, not imagined.

We have six families, including one pregnant woman expecting her first child, four other children and two teenagers.

We have a six-year-old master chess player who is a Ukrainian national treasure. She took subtle delight, though measured in her display of confidence, as she has impeccable manners and clearly didn't want to boast, to beating the socks off Paul. She takes the game of chess quite seriously and yet she had a slightly turned up smile during the game which set the tone from the first move who the winner would be. Poor Paul was massacred. He turned the King on his side. He fell on his sword. Still, she insisted on shaking hands at the finish.

She carries her baby dolls around and makes direct eye contact with you. She doesn't run from anything. She plays the recorder like Zbigniew Preisner.

The women rake leaves, cook and clean with a formidable commitment. There is no hesitation. They make soup like a 15th century alchemist.

I don't know why there are some women who rarely come out of their rooms, the older ones. I don't know whose husband is alive and whose husband is dead. I do know that most have lost their homes and in some cases, they had to leave their pets behind. I don't know about their friends.

I do know that their lives are changed forever. Home is no more. Now they have to cling to each other and rely on the goodness of strangers. They must eventually consider who will be the best host country, who will take them, what language will be the easiest to learn, who will have work. They have the daunting task of rebuilding their lives and perhaps with an incomplete family.

Daria is expecting her first child. A little girl. Daddy is moving around the Ukraine. Will she start off life with him or will she grow up with only stories told about him?

For the past near twenty years I have told the story of Rose and Henry Kieniewicz and how they arrived in Scotland with only the clothes on their backs, without a penny to their names.

Every morning I look into the eyes of this memory, the memory of my mother-in-law, the memory of all who made it out of Poland in 1945 alive. There are half laughs, moist eyes, deep sighs, distant looks.

Every morning, there is something to touch, something real, something tangible, some practicality that needs addressing: a pair of shoes, a needle and thread, a pair of slippers, a bottle brush, cough drops.

Do I pray? Of course I pray. Do I know there are angels around us? Of course I do because there are. I just no longer think about the women as I did the women from Yemen and Syria, whom I thought about with great concern but only thought about, only imagined and theorised about.

Today, I have coffee with these women, the Ukrainian women. And we just sit together. Very few words are exchanged, but the care and the love at that table, the power in it is enough to give birth to a new star. All women and children all over the world who have been forced to flee their homes, their lives because of the tyranny of evil sits in spirit with us.

I will be writing this diary during the week, when time permits. I think it's important.
Amber

Tomorrow: Dignity and Shame. How we receive a Humanitarian Crisis.

Wednesday, March 9, 2022

Vladysłava was relieved today to wake up and learn that her apartment had still not been bombed and her cat was still alive, though hungry. A friend from the West drove to Kharkiv to put food out for her wee creature. Today is good. Two mothers and their children arrived about two hours ago from Sumy where they dodged bullets and bombs to make their connection with a driver who took them to the West where they were able to cross the border into Poland. They are staying for one night before continuing onto Germany.

We have a few local Polish women who work here and one gets on my nerves, badly. She's a good worker as unpleasant as she is, with the exception of stealing alcohol, which I now put under lock and key, as I have said, a good worker. But we live in a small community and being an old Jungian, I remember a story that Marie Louise Von Franz told about when she and her family moved into a small village when she was still just a child.

The neighbour's son came to door to declare that his father was a kleptomaniac, but, otherwise, perfectly harmless. He reassured them that when something went missing to please let him know and he would return it as soon as he found it. As an adult, Von Franz became the leading authority on fairy tales, their meaning, a superior analyst and protege of Carl Jung.

She cites this story because she feels we need to learn how to live together again without labeling each other or institutionalising those who struggle and are challenged within themselves. And as annoying as living next door to a kleptomaniac without limitations must have been, she said her father laughed it off and they lived alongside this peculiarity for quite some time.

It's a successful way to integrate the shadow, and if we are in a small community and accept these things about others, then the collective group is likely healthier.

This story has a point. Today, the woman who annoys me so badly, told Paul that some of the Ukrainian women were helping themselves to too much of the food. There are some things that make me want to lock and load. After all, I am from Texas. I suppose it's in my nature. Fortunately, I have poor vision.

What's on many a mind in the Polish countryside is the story that asks, who among the Ukrainians is rich. Are there Ukrainians who have a car, for example? How much is the car worth? We had four women drive from the Ukraine so their cars are of particular interest. By the way, this is not a foreign topic of conversation in the cities either.

It's an extraordinary phenomenon that the suspicion sets up early. To begin, there is a language barrier. Add to that a lot of assumptions and narrow-mindedness and suddenly, you have an inferior group of people called refugees, immigrants who are going to take away our jobs, our money, overwhelm our cities, and result in the ruination of our economy.

There is an attitude among those who are inclined to such attitudes, for example, to buy the cheapest cuts of meat, the block cheeses with no flavour, mealy apples, and old vegetables, good enough for soup. These refugees don't need anything new; they will survive on donations and canned fish.

Sichów is full of the most interesting people. We have artists, musicians, our little six-year-old chess player, financial planners and probably a teacher or two. In time, I will discover such things about our guests. But for now, they are my guests.

How is it that the human being can so quickly fall into fault-finding, accusation, reproach, denunciation? It must be driven by fear.

That's where dignity and shame come into play. The government doesn't help the situation by any means. And the headmaster of the school next door is upset with us because there has been a border dispute raised about the property since it fell into ruin and was neglected by the communists for decades after the war. I mention this because he acquired several boxes of donations which may or may not have helped us but, at any rate, he moved them on and was asked by a local government employee why he didn't share them with us, he said, it would be because of a border dispute.

The clothes weren't for me.

Thus, I refuse to call them refugees. They are my guests. They are on equal territory and have something to teach me. I can learn from their lives.

When Vladysława was leaving our conversation today she said, "You know, we don't think in terms of dates or days of the week anymore, we think in terms of war. It's been 14 days since the start of the war. Tomorrow will be 15."

(I have only about one hour each day to write these diaries so do forgive if they have mistakes).

March 11, 2022
Day 16

This was the welcome speech at the general meeting yesterday:

I want to welcome each of you and tell you that it is an honour for Paul and I to receive you here at Sichów, here in our home.

We consider you as our guests and we are here to serve you.

As a woman and a mother, I am particularly passionate about your comfort and your well-being. In particular about your specific needs.

I am also very aware of the need for you to maintain your own sense of dignity, way of living and routine, as best as is possible under the circumstances. Paul and I are here to help you with that.

There are a few things that will be discussed today that will hopefully make our lives together a bit more united.

Finally, it is of great importance to me, that for as long as you are here, you feel the freedom of protection and safety for yourselves and for your children.

We are a community now, even if only for a little while or a long while. Being in a community means that every voice is important. Please do not hesitate to ask for what you need and to share your feelings if you so desire.

I have fallen in love with Ukrainian women. I think you are formidable. Thank you for coming into my life.

With great respect. Pani Amber

We achieved a lot as a group, setting up rotas for cooking, keeping the fireplaces stocked and burning, getting the children organised for school and information on passports, visas and so forth.

We offered psychological help, but nobody raised their hand.

Sadly, though, everyone in that meeting is suffering to some degree from PTSD.

I think you will agree how this following development in the community supports my observation.

When I came home today from the store, I was met with Marina who could hardly speak through the floods of tears. She took me upstairs to where her things had clearly been tossed into the hallway. Natasha is the woman with whom she had been sharing a room and the one who threw her things into the hallway. They know each other through Marina's boyfriend, who is Natasha's son. Because of the language barrier, all I could understand was that Marina had been accused of kicking Natasha's dog.

It took me a bit of negotiation to get Marina's phone and her shoes back from the room but when I managed to do so, I relocated her to the Palace where she is spending the next few days. (The Palace is what we call Stefan's house. It's an old 18th century manor home; in Polish, a Dwór.)

One of the things that Marina kept saying over and over again is, 'I can do this. I'm in control, I'm in control, I can do this, I'm in control.'

She is not in control. She is in shock and she is traumatised and now she has jumped on to one of these volunteer sites where people offer to take you to various parts of Europe, usually into cities where there is promised work. She has been offered such a ride to the Netherlands and actually been guaranteed work to which she cannot say what type of work because, in fact, it is non-existent work. She has no permit and would have to register in the Netherlands and follow very tight protocols to enter such a situation. In theory, it would be a good idea for her to be in a city but to run off to where she knows no one is not a good idea. She has no place to stay, no money, no job and knows no one. I think I will ask for a translator and see if we cannot somehow reach some sort of reconciliation together.

I am frightened because of the human trafficking network whose perpetrators pluck young girls from Eastern Europe and Marina is a classic catch. She's 22, wide-eyed, pretty, naive, and comes from a broken home. Her vulnerability makes her an easy target.

I'm very worried about Marina and can only promise to write when I know something more.

I think what strikes me most from the point of view as a witness to the trauma of war and its effect on people is how far reaching and elaborate the system of disruption.

This young girl has now not only escaped the shelling of her neighbourhood in Kharkiv, but her boyfriend has abandoned her in favour of the mother's side of the story. She thinks she is alone but as long as she is here, she is not alone. I can see in her eyes that she's not ready to leave and I want to protect her until we can find a suitable solution. She confessed that she is very nervous and unsettled when there is conflict and all she wants to do is run. And run, and run.

I assured her that conflict, conflict resolution and the finesse of such things can only be learned, they do not come to us naturally. I gave her a warm hug and shared that I am now in my senior years and conflict resolution is still a challenge but I'm learning. There is quite a misconception among the young that everyone else has their life in order, everyone except them. What I did tell her, is that most people on the planet are besieged by internal chaos. She is not alone.

We will see how tomorrow unfolds. Anticipating Day 17.

March 13, 2022
Day 18

We have convinced Marina not to go to the Netherlands, so for the moment she is safe with us as we draft a new plan.

The UK has opened up their borders with fewer restrictions and we have family and friends there so we could place her with a known sponsor. She speaks English which would make finding work easier. I would only place her with a person I know and trust; preferably a woman and a mother who has heretofore had to deal with difficult kids and would be willing to commit to seeing her through to a settled status.

The other English speaking residents who advise me on this matter would rather see her remain here for another month as they are convinced the war will be over soon and everyone will return.

I have no idea if the war will be over in a month. I have my doubts. And besides, as I told them this morning, the entire infrastructure will have to be rebuilt so what kind of life would she have there.

The train stations in Poznań, Warsaw, Wrocław and Kraków (at least these I know for a fact, but likely in Łódź and Lublin too) are jam packed with refugees. There are volunteers who bring food and blankets but these refugees are stacked high and hygiene is a problem, disease spreads easily, altogether it's yet another disaster in the making.

The Polish government had originally offered to hotels and spa resorts 120 pln per day, per refugee for food and shelter. Now, they have reduced that to 40 pln per day and hotels, as a result, will not participate. They can't. It's not enough to shelter and feed and care for the needs of those in such a situation. I don't have an axe to grind with the hotels but the government is downright disgraceful in their decision to cut the per diem rate below sustainability.

We are now at 32 refugees and will likely have more coming. When the weather is warm, we can pitch tents and feed them in the common area and see to their medical needs.

However, this is of no value to those trapped inside train stations all across Poland. The United States (from what I've heard) has given the Polish government one million dollars to house these refugees but their solution is to put them on the floors of abandoned schools and other large community spaces providing only beds.

The fragility of this crisis is no different from any other humanitarian crisis of this kind. The Polish government could mobilise and steward their funds to create a more humane atmosphere; providing beds and an inadequate meal is not enough.

To add insult to injury, there is one place only in the whole of Poland that will exchange Ukrainian money and that's in Warsaw. The exchange rate is poor. To say that the Hryvnia is not worth the paper it's printed on is probably the truth.

We are going to turn the heat on in the Dwór and start accepting more refugees there. Stefan is going to Warsaw in about five days and will be volunteering at the train station. I'm sure he will return with a family.

Today, we have a zoom call with a family friend from London who has a good situation there and can help host a few.

As the day closes on Day 18, we have a stable plan for Marina. She has relatives in Zurich who are willing to shelter and care for her until she can get on her feet.

She will have to take a few courses in German, but we 'vetted' the situation this morning and after a long conversation with the auntie who lives in Zurich is prepared to receive her, we feel confident that Marina's best interest is at heart here.

We will put her on the most direct train or bus to Zurich within the next few days. We will make sure she has some pocket money and, of course, sandwiches.

We will go to the eye doctor tomorrow. Maria needs new glasses. And we will have a doctor make a house call for the new woman who arrived from Kyiv last night in a wheelchair. She is 87 years old and travelled with her daughter. They had no running water and no electricity in Kyiv. It was like that for five days before they decided they had best at least try to make it to the border.

Paul's cousin, Henry, and his dear wife, Yulia, belong to this family and because of their tireless efforts were able to not only bring grandma and auntie through but also the grandchildren.

This is how we work at Sichów; this is what your donations support.

A million thanks.

March 14, 2022
Day 19

Carl Jung said we all walk in shoes too small.

I don't think this applies to Olesya, however. She was up early with her hair beautifully braided, her outfit could have easily been an advertisement for Gap Kids, her teddy bear backpack hung evenly over each shoulder; she was ready to go to school.

Her mother, a friend, me and the dogs accompanied her as she marched up the steps, shoulders squared, into the school office where she waited to be registered. Once the formalities were complete, she marched up another set of stairs into the classroom.

I have mentioned Olesya before. She is our chess champion. She's the one that never averts your stare. I believe she enjoys looking at people. I suspect she studies us. This precious child was lovingly carried through a war zone by an attentive family who treasures her. This is her centre-point. This is the place that informs her, the place from where she situates herself in the world.

Paul drove the teenagers into town where the head mistress of the local high school welcomed them. They returned today full of excitement and hope. They will be studying Polish, astronomy, history of the Ukraine, general history (Poles like history), maths; overall, preparatory classes for their matura, much like the exams American students take before entering university. Two are ballet dancers. One is a budding young filmmaker.

Ukrainians are keen on school. Not even war stops them in their path to an education. I can honestly say I've never seen anything like it. It's natural to them, it has an easiness about it, and you don't feel a tremendous pressure applied from anyone – they just genuinely like school. They like to learn.

Henry and Yulia are here from London. Henry is the son of Paul's first cousin, Magdalena. His wife, Yulia, is Ukrainian. They have been with us for a week on a mission to evacuate four of their family members: Yulia's grandmother, her auntie, and her two cousins.

Each of the four have a chilling story. Each escaped the shelling in Kyiv. First the cousins made their way to the border, walking 20 kilometres with what they could carry, wading through water near waist deep, observing the dead on the side of the road. (In another entry I will tell you about the 'transportation' company that nearly absconded with their money – what little they have – and possibly might have put them in even danger – but later). The world has asked of them to witness too much. Thankfully, Henry and Yulia were waiting at the border and brought them to safety. It looked like they would be leaving mother and grandmother behind for an unknown period of time but when the block of flats was destroyed, the one just next door to them, the neighbour suggested they get out. The same 20 kilometres he pushed the wheelchair over endless stretches of rubble, with Yulia's 87-year-old grandmother holding on tight.

Before they made this journey, they would hide in the basement of the building when the night-time bombing began. One night, her cousin drew a picture of what he would consider the perfect day. A football pitch, the sun shining, his mates, all playing what Americans call soccer. His mother looked down at this paper and she said to herself, *we may die here tonight*. You might never play football again.

But for this family, there is a different ending. They did not die. Mom sat at the table with Yulia last night and expressed her thoughts that now she considered anything possible, all is manageable now that they are safe.

Henry and Yulia are not your typical pair. They have pulled four family members from the jaws of death. They have been the family's ambassadors to peace and safety. No stone has been left unturned. They will continue to work from London, first sorting paperwork for the cousins to join them, and then, in time, mother and grandmother, who will stay with us at Sichów until then.

The doctor will make a house call tomorrow to make sure all are well. Did I tell you that the cousins were adopted by Yulia's auntie? They had lost their parents to war in 2014, in Donetsk.

I will drive Maria to the eye doctor for an examination and new glasses tomorrow.Today, I took her grandfather who literally came with the clothes on his back for a new pair of jeans, a jacket and a pair of tennis shoes. He was most pleased. In fact, we had a impromptu fashion show. He said he felt young again.

We have two blind people and three of their family members arriving tomorrow. They will stay at the Dwór.

We bought Marina's ticket today. She leaves tomorrow. I will miss her but insisted she contact me if anything untoward were to happen. She promised.

I would like to talk about enchantment and mythology. Perhaps tomorrow when I hope to be feeling better. I'm warding off a cold.

One thought I can pass along today is: these Ukrainians have also impacted my life forever. Fear is not a word I will use recklessly ever again. I will think long and hard before I dare resort to such extravagance.

March 16, 2022
Day 21

'... the only real danger that exists is man himself ... and
we know nothing of man – his psyche
should be studied because we are the origin of all coming
evil...' ~ Carl Jung

Henry Straw wrote to me this morning and told me that Nietzsche said we are guided by our own depth, and when we respond to this, we are living our myth. However, he warns us against large ideas. Nietzsche, that is. There is a danger that the insight will come too soon to understand itself. This is what Henry wrote to me this morning.

Henry was the director of the Jung Centre Houston in 1995 when I went to work there. It was a time when the curriculum offered a ten-week course on the Collected Works of Carl Jung. (They don't offer this anymore and not because the current director would oppose, if anything, I'm sure Sean Fitzpatrick would delight to see such an addition but it's not a popular subject and the classes would not fill).There was a visible enthusiasm to talk soul and mythology and dreams and fairy tales. There were so many then who wanted to know why we did the things we did. And when Marion Woodman said with authority, 'Unconscious means unconscious,' we wanted to know what that meant and how to get there: what was this road into the unconscious? What was a complex? What was shadow work? What is the psyche? Is there a God? What is the nature of evil?

Probing these questions, studying material that could help us understand who we are was plentiful and extensive. These courses were challenging and undiluted. I didn't realize it at the time, but those were the golden years.

Lawrence Hillman, James Hillman's son, once told me that his father said to him: 'When you have a problem, make it really big so you can see it.'

I can't think of anything bigger than close proximity to a war to illustrate his remark.

So here's what troubles me today; profoundly so.

It got all stirred up last night when we took in five more people, three of whom are suffering from noticeable trauma, psychological fragility, and an edginess that we are simply not qualified to handle. They have requested to be placed elsewhere. The best we can do at the moment is offer them a private flat in the town that sits empty most of the year. It belongs to a family member of Stefan's who has graciously offered to help us out. Still, I don't know if they will take it and I don't under any circumstances think this is the best solution long term because I believe they need a more advanced level of care.

So this war. How did we get here? I'm sure there's not a shortage of historians who can tell us how we got here politically, but how did we get here spiritually and psychologically?

As I see it, our civilization has put itself at the top of the food chain and thus set off a catastrophic state of affairs leading to acute narcissism, consumerism, restlessness, hyper-anxiety, melodrama, and obsessive rationalization, to name a few symptoms. We live in a world that seeks to intellectualize fairy tales. Ritual is awkward for us and we don't understand what it means to live a symbolic life.

We place everything on the outside of ourselves and are surprised when there's a crisis.

42

But indeed there is a crisis. And up until now, for example, the three suffering souls who arrived last night had been contained within the borders of their everyday lives until war aggressively forced them into a situation that is now untenable for them.

In point of fact though, it's no different from the shooter who emboldens himself one weekday morning, armed and prepared to kill as many as possible. There is a war going on inside of him too, I assure you.

So, what is inside of us? We're so compulsive about what we eat and the supplements we take, and what we look like and how we age and if we get enough exercise, if our Instagram life is successful, if we have a plethora of Facebook friends and on and on but who is it that's inside of us? Whose life are we living?

> ... Today everyone asserts his own personality and strives to live a full life as an individual. But these efforts lead not to a full life but to suicide, because, instead of realizing his personality, man only slips into isolation. For in our age, mankind has been broken up into self-contained individuals, each of whom retreats into his lair, trying to stay away from the rest, hiding himself and his belongings from people and people from him. And, while he accumulates material wealth in his isolation, he thinks with satisfaction how mighty and secure he has become, because he is mad and cannot see that the more goods he accumulates, the deeper he sinks into suicidal impotence ... he has split off from the whole and become an isolated unit; he has trained his soul not to rely on human help ...
> ~ *The Brothers Karamazov*,
> Fyodor Dostoevsky, 1879.

To live our myth yet not to let it overtake us. To always be prepared to practice humility. And the only way I know how to do this is to remain in service to others, even the ones that really get on my nerves. I am actively and consciously in a relationship with something larger than myself. Some bigger story, something wiser and something timeless.

I should have been a Methodist minister ... like Henry!

Saturday, we are all going on a day trip to Sandomierz and having pizza on the way home. We have hired transportation that can seat 26 and we'll add two more private cars to absorb the rest.

March 20, 2022
Day 25

The Ancestors are Watching and The Tears in Vladysłava's Eyes

> The magic of the place you love meant that Sichów, surrounded by a large green clump of trees, seemed like the safest place for us at the time. Every rat in a moment of real danger, if it can, flees to its own well-known hole. There was probably something of that in this decision.
> ~ *Świadetwo Czasu Minionego,* Zofia Skórzyńska (Testimony of a Time Gone By).

In 1944, the three Radziwiłł sisters walked twenty kilometres from Słupia to Sichów after an evacuation order was issued from the Soviets who burst into the basement and told the families there to leave as soon as possible for they were in imminent danger of being re-occupied by the Nazis. The Red Army was at Barnowo, not far from Sandomierz where we were yesterday on our outing. The front line was shifting.

The older girls, including their brother Staś, had been staying in Słupia since their parents had been arrested by the Nazis in 1940; their father taken to Majdanek and their mother to Ravensbruck. Anna, the youngest, was only nine months old at the time and she stayed at Sichów in the care of Fr. Rector Konstanty Michalski.*

---

* Fr. Michalski was the rector at the Jagiellonian University during Sonderaktion Krakau, when he and his colleagues were tricked into the famous Lecture Room 56 where they were seized and taken to the camps by the Gestapo. The Intelligenzaktion or intelligentsia mass shootings, was a

The house that belonged to Krysia and Maciej Radziwiłł is still standing today and functions as a care home. This is where Staś and his sisters stayed up until August, 1944, before the long walk home. (As a matter of note, Staś was grouped together with others who would also make their way to Sichów separately).

When the mother escaping Kharkiv with her blind son and daughter, noticeably affected by trauma, arrived here at Sichów mid-week, we offered to re-house them in a town flat in Staszów. The young woman could not stop remembering the sounds of shelling and explosions, and when she arrived here to see that our property was still in half-ruin, she was undone. It's not often that someone has such an aversion, but given all she had come through, perhaps Sichów was too much of a reminder of the devastation of war. Visible damage left in a state of decay. I felt it was a bad idea to leave them on their own under the circumstances and pushed for another solution. We called Pan Grzegorz, a Ukrainian native who speaks Polish, with whom we consult quite frequently these days. He and Stefan drove to the convent in Pacanów. The sisters indicated they might be able to help.

---

mass murder scheme conducted by Nazi Germany against Polish intelligentsia, devised early in the war for the sole purpose of eradicating the Polish elite. There were upward of 180 professors, lecturers and employees of the university arrested that day in November of 1939 and all were dispersed first to Sachsenhausen then later to Dachau and Buchenwald. Fr. Michalski was among them.

After an international protest by prominent Italians, among them Mussolini and the Vatican, the Reich was forced to begin a strategy of release. Fr. Michalski and a group of other professors made their way to Sichów for shelter.

When they opened the door, there was a larger than life (or so it seemed to Stefan at the time) framed photograph of his great aunt and uncle, Krysia and Maciej Radziwiłł, alongside a sizeable plaque thanking them for their generosity in funding the convent not only after the war but throughout the remainder of their lives.

When I heard the story that night, I knew this family would be in the protective space of those who were certainly better qualified to support and serve them.

The living presence of our ancestors had guided them to safety.

The magic of Sichów.

Every nerve ending in my body stands on alert. My life will never be quite the same again as my choices will be now be informed by this experience. Do I need it, can I live without it, is there something more important I could be doing, am I making a difference in my household by the decisions I make?

The nuance and subtleties of the everyday are particularly poignant. The feeling that overtakes me when I consider all of us living under one roof, each and every wounded one of us, emerging from our rooms, some irritated, frustrated, overwhelmed, frightened, remote, exhausted, restless and angry, how we all swirl together in this space co-creating our lives, after a single twist of fate has thrown us together against our will by the hardship of war.

Yesterday, we went to Sandomierz in a hefty van that seated 26. Paul and I took another car to carry the remainder.

The sun was high in the sky and even though it wasn't very warm, it was beautiful. We walked around town for a couple of hours. We had ice cream. We looked in shop windows. We sat in the main square and watched the children play. Then, pizza and the drive home.

I was hoping for a reprieve but we got a call that a family in distress needed a place to stay. Fortunately, we have two young men under the age of 18 who are capable of moving beds and mattresses, and one of the ladies who work for us sprung into action with clean sheets and towels so that by five o'clock, we were ready for their arrival. Paul and I rested and then met the bus from Warsaw at eight.

We haven't gotten to know our new family yet; they will likely decompress for a few more days. The father has had brain cancer and is traveling with his wife, two children and mother. He is not well and neurologically; his illness is obvious. They crossed the border in early March and were right away put into a large stadium without privacy or adequate toilet services, poor hygienic conditions and food without much nutritious value. They got sick. They left the stadium and returned to the train station platform. At least there, they could find a place of warmth. This is where Stefan met them yesterday. He volunteers there when in Warsaw. They were on their way to Łodz. Apparently, they had a little money left and found a hotel they could afford and decided to spend it for a good night's sleep. Thankfully, they are now here. I can't even imagine what would have become of them with no money and no relatives outside of the Ukraine.

I'm a long way from my conversation with my cousin, Basia, earlier in the week when we were talking about her friend from choir who is a Ukrainian cook-book author and is responsible for raising funds for the soldiers. We were talking about how women move through the world during a crisis, what they hold sacred. And in some cases, what a civilization holds valuable.

For 200 years, Poland did not exist as a separate nation. They kept their identity through their language, folk art and food. With a houseful of Ukrainian women who are always cooking, walking dogs, running after children, cleaning and speaking in their native language, I am reminded of the resolve of the Sichów ancestors.

One woman told me that if I could say only one word in their language, it would be 'borscht', not soup, but borscht. This is the defining word when remembering the Ukrainians, when beginning to understand who they are.

It made me think of the tears in Vladyslava's eyes when a relative from Russia tells her that the Ukrainians are murdering themselves; that Russians have nothing to do with this war. And no matter what she says to defend her position, they have made up their minds that she is, in fact, the perpetrator.

I am afraid for the Ukraine. I am afraid their borders will disappear and they will have to go on the run for years to come, holding onto their language, their folk art, and their borscht.

Tomorrow we will shop for curtains for the nursery. We will also take Andrzej with us as he needs trousers.

One of the women said to me this morning that yesterday in Sandomierz was 'joy', no, in fact, she said, 'it was joyful.' It is true that our visit was restorative and we are planning another outing, this time to Krakow in two weeks.

March 24, 2022
Day 29

Yesterday, I spent the better part of the day in a processing centre for Ukrainians who are being sponsored by UK families or joining their own families already re-settled. It was an impressive set- up in a modern office building in Rzeszów city centre. The visa application department of Sheffield sent a dozen or so volunteers to assist in this massive relocation plan. It was well organized, friendly, with plenty of water and fruit *and* toys on hand for the children, while these tireless case workers attended to each group. There were upward of one hundred people filing through and according to the gentleman who worked with us, it was about an average number per day.

There are over two million Ukrainian refugees in Poland. Of course, not all will stay. And nobody knows how long the war will last and what will be left upon return. Who will be in the market to rebuild? Who will have the stamina, who will not? For the moment, though, some are here taking shelter and making a plan.

Sichów has been a place of rare occurrence as it has allowed its residents an opportunity to recharge. They have a private space with an ensuite bathroom, nutritious food, on site administrative assistance to advise with their documents, access to medical care, medicine, new shoes and clothes. *And* toys for the children. This is possible because of our generous donors from around the globe. The Polish government gives us 40 złoty a day per person – for now.

However, today we experienced an exodus. Room 1 and 6 have moved on to The Netherlands and we understand that Room 11 is right behind them. Of course, there are hundreds, if not thousands in line for these rooms which will be prepared for the next uprooted, traumatized family, in need of legitimate care, but my heart is feeling the great sadness of one who stays behind fully conscious of the unpredictability these families will encounter along the way. (Let me pause here and redefine the word family for you. These are mothers and children traveling alone. There are no fathers, brothers husbands, only women and their babies. It is necessary to visualize this in order to understand the impact).

I'm not so grandiose as to think that Sichów can be all things to all people; that would certainly be an ego inflation. It's just that I can't stop crying again. When the house was full and those in it at a temporary stopping point in their diasporic journey, there was an odd sense of peace, a kind of Arcadian bliss, a pastoral atmosphere where we all perceived ourselves safe from the horror of war and the evil that relentlessly pursues. Like a sweet dream.

But our situation is otherwise. It is an image of women and their children on the run from a beast, a monster who cannot be satisfied; in fact, so dissatisfied is he that he murders pregnant women and women at their most sacred hour, when giving birth. He thinks this will satisfy his hunger.

This is our world. And it has been for a very long time.

When I lived in Scotland, I remember a story that came out of the Iraq war. It was a bus load of twenty or so women coming back from work. They were intercepted by a tribe of one affiliation or other and beheaded each and every one. One was pregnant. That night, Mama didn't come home. Nor did a daughter, a wife, an auntie, a sister or a friend.

This is our world. There is something in me that chooses to weep because the rage is so great and I don't know what to do with that, so I will cry and I will keep buying cake and toys for the children. The new ones. The ones on the road already have a doll to carry. That comforts me greatly.

I know that what is happening today is another chapter in the book of nationalistic ideologies and that doesn't really help me figure this out psychologically because I am mad and everything in me wants to protect and restore to its rightful place a woman who makes broth for her sick child. Women seek many a path today so I must mind myself that I don't stereotype us. But I feel we are in danger of losing values that historically have been associated with women.

When will it be enough for those who have enough but continue to consume? Will there ever be a time again when domestic life is appreciated, enjoyed and treasured for what it is? Hard to say. It's not a question to pose to an inner city single mother raising children on a minimum wage. Nothing terribly appealing about that, is there?

So this is our world. What do we value? When will we change? When will we wake up to a more superior consciousness than what social media represents?

As I write this entry, we have already had a call to receive a woman, a grandmother and two children with no money on the platform in Warsaw. They will be coming tomorrow. Infrastructures, attitudes, values, will have to creatively change in order for there to be a chance at a new consciousness. We are living in a fatherless world. We lost our fathers during the Industrial Revolution to machines and now we are losing them to war. The inner cities are plagued by the absence of a father who is fully present in his child's life. I can't bear to think of those Ukrainian men who will not be coming home again. But this is part of the reality of war.

John Hill writes in *At Home in the World*:

Obviously, there are vast differences in the social circumstances of the privileged few who can derive much satisfaction in transiting from one culture to another, when compared with economic or political immigrants. No doubt the privileged have problems of their own; nevertheless, they and their dependents receive ample help in making necessary adjustments–many international schools and social faculties are professionally geared to alleviate the pains of cultural change and cultural loss. Far worse is the plight of economic or political immigrants who have been forced to leave their original homeland. They begin their new life in a state of disorientation, often without any adequate aid in readjustment, and are usually unwelcome or stigmatized. Slums and ghettos, racism, and sex tourism express some of the ugly living conditions of millions of men, women, and children who are forced to live in transitional spaces due to political persecution, the need for economic survival, or the destabilizing effects of exploitation of their land and culture by the richer nations of the industrial world. It has become increasingly difficult for immigrants from the Third World to achieve equal status with the citizens of their host country.

Paul and Stefan and I are seriously considering something more than care for these residents and once we have a plan in place, I will let you know.

Meanwhile, we open our rooms, our kitchen and our hearts to new women and children who need to regroup, rest and reset.

March 27, 2022
Day 32

Natasha is from the Dnipro area of the Ukraine. She speaks both Russian and Ukrainian but I think most of the time she is speaking Russian. She is a force. Her dark, flashing eyes are quick to size up a situation. For example, on the morning after her late night arrival she right away noticed the Orangerie (the room filled with donations) and didn't hesitate a minute to collect a bag of things for her family. It is rare to see a man traveling with the women, but her son has brain cancer so was permitted leave for medical reasons. He's 37. His wife and two children are also with him. Natasha wasn't here but three days before she commandeered the kitchen as her own. She enlisted Iryna as her deputy and together they made what the Poles call pierogi ruskie (potato and cheese filled dumplings), sausages wrapped in a yeasty dough, and a pot of mashed potatoes that stood the size of an average three-year-old.

I couldn't imagine what in the world she was planning to do with all those potatoes until the next day when she swept through the kitchen boasting a plate full of mince stuffed potato patties that had been deep fried. I think they're called zrazy. And I want her to sell them. We have a window in the kitchen that was open and selling burgers to the students in the village before the virus; this window would be perfect for Natasha. It's like a metaphor, this window. She opens it and something of her sorrow, her experience now of exile, the broken heart of a mother with a sick child, her traditions are exchanged hand to hand. Let not her creative offering be eclipsed or hidden away because of the cruel and vicious circumstance of war; no, Natasha is not a 'nonperson.'

Historically, the table was the central nervous system of the house. It was usually in front of the fire place where the cooking was done. In fairy tales, it's prominent; as is food and cooking and feasting.

When we celebrate together, we typically cook and dine together. We break bread together. We drink wine together. We share our recipes. We restore ourselves from sickness to health with a warm bowl of bouillon or a cup of herbal tea.

Over the years, however, the table has come to serve as more of a decorative feature in the modern home. I am not implying that there are not those who don't still cook for themselves and serve at table, but with the advent of restaurants and take out options including delivery of prepackaged foods, the table has become more versatile, not carrying the same psychological weight of times past. Certainly, not the same mythology. It's function is not exclusively a place to gather and eat but now doubles as a place of work, a place where we can stack our mail, papers, books and other non-food items.

With the rise of the machine and the modernization of our daily lives, we have demythologized our cultural habits. To see a lineage of women in a house such as grandmother, mother, daughter, sharing in the responsibilities of the household duties is a rare sight. And where this lineage is evident, it's often uprooted by war and the genocidal impact of war leading to complete disruption and ultimate exile.

This is only one aspect of the domestic life, heretofore, cared for by women which has been endangered for the whole of my adult life. The table as the central nervous system, as the central gathering place, as the heart of the household.

The table has also been threatened by extreme poverty in some countries. I remember a book that took me by storm called *Evicted: Poverty and Profit in the American City*, by Matthew Desmond. This book offers an unequivocal, unflinching portrait of the inner-city public housing disaster in major cities in America. In it he writes, 'If poverty persists in America, it is not for lack of resources. We lack something else.'

I realize it must seem I am far afield from Sichów and the resident women living and cooking and creating as best of a temporary life here as is possible.

Not at all. What is happening around the globe, is a war on women and it's not exclusive to the Ukraine. Women and children are forced into exile daily, either because of a strong military presence enforcing school closures, or no running water, are put out of their homes because of non-payment leaving them out in the cold with nowhere to go; food shortages, the stories are literally countless and it is the most vulnerable among us affected.

What is it, the something we lack as a civilization? How is it that this problem continues to escalate with no stoppage in sight? Women are struggling everywhere and there are few foundational support systems in place that protect them or that restore them when they have been compromised. And I haven't even touched upon the subject of human trafficking but you can count on there being young victims of this sort of exploitation resulting from the war in the Ukraine where families have been forcefully torn apart.

Inna is our resident grandmother's daughter. She is the sister of the one who made the harrowing journey from Kyiv with their mother who went into hospital the day after she arrived. Inna lives in the U.K. and is preparing the documents necessary to relocate them both. Inna hadn't seen her mother since last April when she was in Kyiv, visiting. She arrived to Sichów yesterday. When she walked into the hospital, her mother said, 'Did you bring the chicken?'

Food and how we depend upon it, how it informs our family traditions, our relationships, and our memories. The table. The place where we cry, laugh, eat, celebrate, argue, share friendships, where we bond with each other, where intimacy is central, this is what we bring with us into exile, what travels with us everywhere we go. From generation to generation, it is the food, the recipes, the traditions that we long to preserve.

There is not a day that passes when I don't feel tremendous privilege in the presence of these women who come together every day around the table.

I will stop here for today as there is so much to say on the subject of food and the table.

I don't often say it, but your prayers really do hold us together here. Thank you.

March 29, 2022
Day 34

> For the good of society, should cosmetic facelifts
> be prohibited? Are they a crime against humanity?
> What you do to your visible image has societal
> implications. Your face is the Other for everyone else.
> If it no longer bares its essential vulnerability, then
> the grounds for caring, the demand for honesty, the
> call to respond on which societal cohesion rests have
> lost their originating source. *The Force of Character,*
> James Hillman.

The call to respond. There is no one here who's face has
been cosmetically altered. Visible on each one is the
disturbance and the surprise of war. Their vulnerability
exposed, there is no filter.

In one sentence I can tell you that Daria's husband
is now here with us at Sichów, though I will not be able
to say how he managed or by what means. When he
came to my room last night, the face of relief greeted
me. A mixture of relief, gratitude, disbelief, wonder, was
all at once discernible. Daria, on the other hand, had
only one distinguishing emotion coursing through her
entire body and that was the overwhelming presence
of joy. The human spirit, its will, had prevailed over
death and destruction and war; at least in this story.

Earlier in the day, Y. came running up to Paul
looking for a ride to Warsaw. Her tear-stained face,
unmistakably anxious. She wants to run vests and
protective gear to the other side of the border. This is a
frequent activity from what I understand but I have no
idea the risks involved. What I do know, is the impulse
to do such a thing is driven by desperation and fear.

Not everyone will survive this war, which means that at some future celebration, some wedding, some baptism, some Easter Sunday morning, a family member will be noticeably missing. There will be more graves and more grief and more tears with each passing day. How do we know the fate of all the brothers, fathers, uncles and husbands related to the women here? The likelihood that one of these women will be left widowed with a fatherless child is highly probable. Thus, Y. does what she can. In a moment of helplessness and despair she runs military supplies to those she can.

Iryna's blood pressure has been running high since she ran out of medicine. She waited to tell us and then had to go to the doctor yesterday morning. I wish she had come earlier to us but at least it's been resolved for the time being. The call to respond. Without one word spoken, through hand gestures and a look of disquiet, her need for help was conveyed.

Before bedtime, Marina came knocking at the door to our room. She was visibly agitated. Something was wrong with Danilo, her five-year-old boy. He had a high temperature and she had no medicine. Paul leapt into action, grabbed the children's acetaminophen and joined her at her quarters. I jumped into the car to warm it up because she was insistent on going to the hospital. But after about twenty minutes, his temperature was going down even though Paul said Marina was a mess and that every move the child made she would jump up and hover over him. Paul was finally successful in convincing her that the medicine would work, and with rest he should be fine. Even Danilo said, 'Mama, please let me sleep. I just want to sleep.' From what I understand, it was a sleepless night for Marina, but Danilo is feeling better this morning.

The call to respond. Marina's husband has had brain surgery, three times. The neurological damage has left him with a face that doesn't ever change expression. I can't imagine what it's like to be in this situation with two children, one sick, and a husband who is limited and unable to make decisions.

Everyone is looking for work. It's the topic of discussion at the table, it's the look of apprehension on everyone's face.

We are developing a work program here but it takes time. We are looking to provide one that will make integration for our residents as seamless as possible. Ideally, a work study program whereby one can also learn the language and then leave with references when the time comes to do so. It's very important because there is already an emerging resentment among the locals where our residents are concerned. The Ukrainians are offered free public transportation. In my own home, there is the occasional raised eyebrow because I buy good jam for the table. Today, one of the women who work here declared how much work there was and when I asked what I could do to lessen or redistribute duties, she suggested I put the residents to work. (Without pay, of course). I asked what would she have them do? They already clean their own rooms and bathrooms, they cook for themselves and they clean up the kitchen afterwards, they rake leaves and are altogether most helpful; did she have a particular idea in mind. The windows, she blurted out. The windows, I mused. We do the windows only twice a year. It's quite a job and we usually hire others to help. So we do. Besides, she muttered, it's going to rain tomorrow.

I am growing in my faith in a way I never saw coming. I am learning to actually trust. I am learning a deeper patience. I have lowered my expectations to a level that allows me to be more open hearted with those who cannot.

April 2, 2022
Day 38

> Charity is what puts order into human activity.
> Utmost charity is the special gift and ripe fruit of
> contemplative prayer. And for those of us who are
> trying to access this level of participation in the
> divine plan, at this point in history, there probably is
> no sharper cutting edge than your own commitment
> – unto death if necessary – to the pursuit of the
> divine companionship, and simultaneously with it,
> comes a spiritual *companioning* with everyone else
> in the human family, even to the point of sharing
> their suffering. ~ Father Thomas Keating.

Father Keating goes on to define for us the etymology
of the word, 'companioning' which has its root in
Latin. 'com' meaning with, or to accompany and 'panis'
meaning bread. A comrade who shares bread with
another.

My nephew Jordan, came from Houston, Texas, to
help us. He cleans rooms, chops wood, accompanies
me on my daily/twice daily trips into town for food
and medicines.

Natalia, our daughter from the UK arrived last night,
also with the intent to help. As has Adam, another
nephew, come to help from Scotland.

Jon and Johanna, another daughter and her husband
are coming but are stuck in London on the runway with
our two granddaughters.

It has been a particularly difficult week organising
one family who is resettling in London. It was an
Olympian achievement on both sides. It took the efforts
of those working from within the UK and from us

here, to fast track visas, rustle up scouts to collect the documents, arrange for a driver willing to risk heavy snow on a seven hour return journey to get the visa here in time for a next day flight, arranging for the ambulance and the accompanying nurse. This is our 87-year-old grandmother who heroically endured the suffering of a ten mile escape from Kyiv before reliable transportation appeared; pushed over rubble, lifted over floods of water in some places, and goodness knows what else, companioned by her daughter and a friend. She spent about ten days in the hospital upon her arrival here and then, when released a few days ago, was medically partnered on her trip to London. I understand she is resting and is well.

Last night, around three in the morning, a commercial sized bus delivered two families within whose members are disabled. This bus is identified as one carrying refugees which indicates a level of protection, I presume, as they drove from Dnipro with a stop in Kyiv to get here. At least the corridors are open, unlike those in and out of Mariupol.

It is bright yellow and big. On the bus were children with Down Syndrome, severe Autism, and Epilepsy. Some will need passage to Warsaw where they can take advantage of a skilled facility for those who are in need of medication and nursing care. Others who are more stable might choose to stay here. These are early days for our new arrivals, but whatever their decision, we will companion them.

Being in service to another is prayer in action. It is not something that comes easily all the time. Among the volunteers who rode with the families through the Ukraine last night, some woke up this morning in tears. Some of this is stress, disbelief, some of it is fear; overall, a sense of unease. It is very difficult to live in 'the day to day' of the utmost charity. One is in an environment of unyielding interruption which requires immediate attention and, more often than not, split decisions. Because these decisions must be made in haste, the people making them are usually themselves tense with a tendency to impatience which can lead to an occasional outburst. For example, last night upon receiving the call from the service looking for space for these families, our decision had to be made quickly as there were rooms to clean, beds to assemble, linen, blankets and pillows to amass. It boiled down to the placement of people in each room. There were three chiefs on the job who didn't necessarily see eye to eye on how it should be organised for the ultimate, most favourable outcome.

Not to mention, it was already approaching seven in the evening when tempers are short anyway after a long day of chores. This is when the larger call to duty must emerge as there is absolutely no space, nor time for conflicting egos. The call to charity is far too precious, too sacred to corrupt it with our single-minded pettiness. The plan was established with relatively little fuss, allowing us to get down to the business of companioning; of sharing their suffering.

I was hoping to tell you all about Bear but this must wait until the next entry. The residents call him Misha, but Jordan and I call him Bear.

The story of Bear is about belonging, at least that's how Jordan sees it.

But now, more family members have arrived. Róża, her husband, Maciej and their daughter, Lusia who declared as she was exiting the car: 'I am one of the most grateful people to have a family like I have.' Lusia is six. (We're indeed grateful for her, too).

We were just in the kitchen making coffee and were talking about prayer. Róża and her family have just come back from Italy where her husband was doing archival research. He is the head of the department of Croatian Studies at the Jagiellonian University in Krakow. She told me how she felt so uncomfortable traveling to Italy, so beautiful and serene while things back here are in such chaos with so many suffering . Then she said, this is a time for prayer. This is what I can offer until I get back and can continue to help.

Prayer. In the spirit of Thomas Merton, 'this listening, this questioning, this humble, and courageous exposure to what the world ignores about itself'. ~ The Climate of Monastic Prayer.

April 7, 2022
Day 43

Diana is born! Mother and baby are doing well, but because of virus restrictions still in place, Igir was not allowed into the birthing room. He waited here at Sichów like one who waits at a mobile phone park for an arriving flight, full of anticipation and excitement. I saw him only minutes after the news and he could hardly form a sentence he was so overjoyed. Another interesting detail about Igir is he shares our last name: Kieniewicz, except with a Ukrainian spelling. Paul's uncle was Poland's national historian after the war, Stefan Kieniewicz, and his son, Janek, followed in his footsteps so naturally Paul called him to see if there was a possible chance this might be a distant relative. As Janek explains it, there was a branch of the Kieniewicz who split off from those in the Kresy (where Paul's father's side of the family was from) in the 19th century and migrated to what is now the Ukraine. The Kresy or what is more commonly known as 'Borderlands' was the Eastern part of the second Polish Republic during the inter-war period, located in what is now Belarus.

I have thus designated myself Ciocia Amber, which delights me to no end.

The bus load of arrivals from Saturday have decided to stay. The children seem to be settling in and they can receive the medical attention they need in Staszów. Paul has already accompanied one of the children and her mother to see the doctor. I can report good results from this first visit.

We have a new baby and a new puppy. Bear also called Misha by the residents because it's a Slavic word for 'teddy bear'. Bear is a hulking presence that started showing up at Sichów a few weeks ago. I had no idea that the children here had already discovered him and were very sad that he appeared to have no home. There were nights when it was cold and raining and he whimpered under the windows of a few who heard him. I hadn't the first notion of any of this. Not long after though, I saw him myself loping across the lawn. One of the workers here said he belonged to a villager but when I inquired further it turned out he had been abandoned.

Paul wasn't thrilled to acquire another dog as we have two plus the cat, but Bear was particularly persuasive when it came to taking up residency at Sichów. Jordan and I finally took him to the vet where we were quite surprised to learn he was near death's door and he's barely a year old. The next few days we spent hours in the office holding him while they gave him fluids, medicines and injections. After his treatment on the third day we came home to wait and see. It was a tense weekend because he wasn't eating much at first and when he finally did devour a whole bowl full, he collapsed into lethargy. I went to bed crying because I really thought we were going to lose him. But the next morning Jordan texted to say he was bounding with energy. Bear now belongs at Sichów. He is a permanent resident.

Bear belongs.

As humans, we long to belong don't we? I can't believe it's much different for a dog who once travelled in a wolf pack. It was where he belonged.

My world is enlarging to include Bear and a new family of residents whose lives were split apart, severed from everything they knew, everything that was familiar, but fortunately not everything they loved.

Yesterday, Andrei showed us his artwork. A few days after his arrival here he pulled a USB stick from his pocket and said: 'My whole life's work is here on this stick. Everything else is lost.' Andrei is an illustrator and designs book covers for a living. He has also written several books on the technique of drawing; the human body, landscapes and famous architectural landmarks. I asked him yesterday if he had ever taught at the university. 'No,' he said, 'I am a practical artist.'

He works primarily in pencil though we did see some paintings. There were a series of detective stories he illustrated and on the cover of one was a very handsome young man. 'This is his son' he said. I can only conclude that he is still in the Ukraine fighting against occupation.

When I woke up this morning to get coffee, Andrei was in the kitchen. I wanted to tell him how he and the presence of his family have changed my life, have forced me to look deeply into what it means to be human, to suffer but also to rejoice. How I value life in a way I never imagined possible. I am so sorry they are here under these circumstances, but that we are and that we manage is what is exceptional about being human. I am learning the great lesson of not taking myself so seriously; of recognizing my own smallness and self-centredness.

When Andrei, laughs he is really laughing. He laughs from his gut. He laughs with abandon.

Our days here together are dedicated to each other. We form a community of human beings.

On Saturday we are heading for another field trip, this time to Krakow. Plus the work study program has begun. It's spring here at Sichów and all is in bloom. Seeds are being sown in the greenhouse, trees are beginning to leaf, the small white wildflowers are visible as far as the eye can see. We are now able to employ several women thanks to the generous donations of our global friends.

There is still yet so much to tell you about the soul of Sichów and how the broken find relief here. I will think about this on the bus ride into Kraków.

April 11, 2022
Day 47

> Because of its fascination evil has considerable power over the human soul, so much power, in fact, that C.G. Jung once aptly commented that only two things could keep a person's soul from falling under the power of evil: if a person's soul is filled with a power greater than the power of evil, or if a person is contained in a warm, related human community. Jung once wrote to William W., a founder of Alcoholics Anonymous, 'I am strongly convinced that the evil principle prevailing in this world leads the unrecognized spiritual need into perdition, if it is not counteracted either by real religious insight or by the protective wall of human community. An ordinary man, not protected by an action from above and isolated in society, cannot resist the power of evil.' ~ *Evil: The Shadow Side of Reality*, John Sanford.

I have come to the conclusion that to ask the question, why are there those who are capable of such egregious acts against their fellow man is the wrong question to ask because this question has no answer. Nor can one answer why another human being can bring himself to commit outright murder, more specifically commit genocide against an entire community based on nothing more than a simple willingness to do so.

The wrong question, in this instance, has no answer.

Mythologically, in parable, through story, rhyme, song and tale only are we able to make sense of human cruelty. In the Gospel of Thomas, Jesus said: "The father's kingdom is like a person who had [good] seed.

His enemy came at night and sowed weeds among the good seed. The person did not let them pull up the weeds, but said to them, 'No, or you might go to pull up the weeds and pull up the wheat along with them.' For on the day of the harvest the weeds will be conspicuous and will be pulled up and burned."

Theologically, 'father's kingdom' as it is written in this parable would indicate the world of matter and not paradise or the world of spirit as it might otherwise be understood when speaking of such a kingdom. In God's world, then, there is evil. In the world of matter. The enemy comes at night to sow the weeds. There is the act of evil and the concept of evil. An example of the act of evil is the intentional destruction of a place, including its inhabitants. The concept of evil is how we come to terms with this act.

Most of our residents took the day trip to Kraków on Saturday. We left the bus and walked across the road together into the town square. There, we decided to identify the restaurant before splitting off into smaller groups for sightseeing. As we were approaching the restaurant location, I noticed a man talking to one of the women in our group. I walked over to him and asked if he spoke English. He did. Then I asked if he knew her. No. He did not. This is when I knew he was a predator. At which point, my voice became very angry and confrontational, asking why he was talking to her as he had no business doing so. To which he replied, 'I am opening a new firm in Kazimierz.'

'Oh I bet you are,' I said.

'I am looking for Ukrainians.'

'Oh I bet you are,' I repeated. Then I told him firmly to get the hell away from our group and to leave us alone. He wanted to give her his email address and I said, no, give it to me. I will take it. He was bold enough to ask who I was to which I replied, 'None of your damn business.' He gave me an email address, which of course was fake. Weeds among us.

Our cousin met us at the restaurant and when I told her the story, she said there are reports of kidnappings in broad daylight. Yesterday, Paul sent me an article about teenagers traveling alone from the Ukraine into London who are being lured into the sex trade. Weeds among us.

Max is leaving us today because he was able to get a Canadian passport. He still has to get it stamped before he can go, but can't get through the throngs of people in Warsaw who literally sleep outside the embassy waiting for the chance to be at the front of the line when the doors do open. Every time he has tried, there are about five hundred people stacked on top of each other waiting to be called. It's impossible at the moment to get what he needs here in Poland, but there is a chance he might fare better in Rome, so he is heading there.

Max is Igir's good friend. We were standing in the coffee area this morning, saying goodbye. I couldn't help myself. I started to cry and then I said to the boys, 'Please forgive me, but I can't stop the tears today. I just simply can't.'

When I think of how an individual can formulate sophisticated schemes of corruption, exploitation, manipulation, lies and harm specifically designed to bring injury against another, I cannot process the thought.

The other day I heard that one of the stores here in Staszów fired two of their Polish employees with the express purpose of hiring two Ukrainians because they get a sizeable benefit from doing so.

All of these stories swirl around inside of me as I'm saying goodbye to Max, apologizing for the tears.

Our guests welcomed the opportunity to talk about what they were feeling too. Igir said that before the war, he thought about a new car, his job, holidays, buying jewellery for his wife, going out with friends, nothing special he said but now all seems meaningless as all he thinks about now is life. Is his wife healthy? The baby? Are they out of harm's way? When he hears a car backfire, he jumps because he will always hear the bombs dropping, the sound of gunfire.

Max does not want to go. Not really. Yes, he recognizes the good fortune of having contacts and resources to begin again, but he is also aware of the road that lies ahead of him, the one without his country. He will be in exile for the foreseeable future.

I was telling them about Paul's family, scattered out around the world after WWII. His father didn't come back to Poland until fifty years later. About the Nazis here at Sichów taking Stefan's grandparents to the concentration camps. About Basia and Bogus's mother who was arrested as an eighteen-year-old, tried and taken to Siberia. Her crime? She was Polish and she lived in what is now the Ukraine and the Russians wanted to cleanse the communities of Polish speaking residents and populate the area with only Russians. Sound familiar? Paul tells me just this moment they are carting people off from Mariupol.

Paul's parents and their contemporaries, cousins, siblings, aunts and uncles managed to create new lives. They re-settled and had children and their children have since had children and so it goes, the generations beget the next.

Zoia is walking outside. I can see her from my window. She should be walking outside her own home somewhere in Kharkiv.

Max and Igir should be going to work there today. What's wrong with dreaming about buying your wife a nice piece of jewellery? What's wrong with planning a vacation or dreaming about an adventure? This question does have an answer and it is nothing, nothing in the world is wrong with this.

The weeds don't grow there. They grow elsewhere. They grow in the heart before they manifest in the mind to become an action.

What are our actions? Mary Magdalene could not stop the crucifixion of Jesus. But she could anoint him with oil. She could not have prevented his death, but she did have the courage to walk with him to his end. In the last Holy Hour of his life, in the Garden of Gethsemane, the inevitability of his death could not be altered, but the love he felt in his heart was his own to express.

There is not a saint, humanitarian, disciple or mystic among us who has not experienced what St. John of the Cross describes as 'the dark night of the soul'. In fact, we who are ordinary also experience these confrontations with the unconscious. John Sanford reminds us of what Jung called the lifelong process that aims at fulfilment, the process of 'individuation', in which the conscious mind and the unconscious mind are acting in unison and not in opposition to each other.

The weeds grow here. In the minds of those who are unconscious. And as painful as it is to accept that we are helpless against this phenomenon, we can fortify ourselves by observing our own actions, our own hearts and following the precept of the Yoga Sutras of Patanjali - *First Do No Harm.*

April 16, 2022
Day 52

Jews will eat unleavened bread at Passover to symbolise their exodus from Egypt. In their haste to freedom, the ancient Hebrews didn't have enough time to wait for the bread to rise.

But they still ate bread in the form of what we would call today, crackers or Matzos. They were practical. There was no waste.

My favourite Rabbi was Reb Zalman Schachter-Shalomi. Before he died, he and his very close friend, Father Thomas Keating walked together to talk about God. It was a sensible conversation about the next generation and where will they take things when they feel so much that they have to move from the outside to the inside. Father Keating says:

> Prayer of the heart presupposes some movement of trying to translate the symbols of the liturgy to some kind of experiential touch or awakening of the mystery that is present ... it's not a good idea to get rid of ritual altogether, but to go through it, not around it, leads you to the mystery contained there, to which it points.

Reb Zalman offered his thoughts: "The people saw and they went backward but Moses went into the dark fog where God could be found. '... the lord is in his holy temple. Be silent before Him all the earth.'

What does it mean to feel so much that one is compelled to go from the outside to the inside and what does that have to do with the residents here at Sichów? I cannot say directly what it has to do with the residents here because I don't know specifically what troubles them. What I do know is that each of us have been thrust together in a destiny none of us could have ever imagined before the war. (Before the war, by the way, is a common expression in Poland used to delineate what had once been a life of dreams and possibilities to what became a life of hardship and unthinkable loss. I was told that Marek Rostworowski said to his daughter, "Everything that was sweet was before the war, is no more."

Yulia and her son arrived on Wednesday night, late. She was coming from Zaporozhye by bus, train and foot before she was collected at the border. Her son was visibly distressed. She had to leave behind her mother who stayed to care for the elderly grandmother who was not strong enough to make the journey. According to Yulia, there is fighting in this area. "Does she have a husband?" I asked Paul, who replied, "I don't know. I don't ask those kinds of questions."

On the same day, we found out that Sasha, Natasha's son, has an inoperable brain tumour and was declined chemotherapy because his iron levels are not good. He is not strong enough to withstand the treatment. The doctor wrote out a prescription for hospice care but our preference is that he be cared for here. He is only 36 years old.

I took Katya to the vet on Friday because she had found a tick on her dog and wanted to get medicine right away. I thought we were just going to run over and get the tablets but she climbed into the car with the dog. When we got to the clinic, Katya took her dog right into the examination room. She was in there for about thirty minutes, most of this time I presume was spent in translation. (We use our phones a lot for this). When she emerged, she was clearly holding back tears. I was very confused. She insisted on paying for the medicine herself and before we could even get to the door, she had to sit in the waiting room chair because she was so overcome by emotion. I finally managed to get her into the backseat of the car and together we spent another thirty minutes in translation, tears and embrace. I held her for a long time. When she calmed down, she said I was like Babcia. Pani Babcia Amber. (Babcia means grandmother in Polish, Baba or Babusia in Ukrainian).

The vet told her that she would give her the medicine for ticks and fleas but, even so, with medicine, there was a chance the dog would die in ten days.

This dog is Katya's lifeline. She escaped with this dog, her son and her mother all the way from Kharkiv. "Pani Amber. I don't know what I would do if my little dog died. She is eleven years old and I love her so much." Poor Katya happened to have a run in with a woman who is probably a good veterinarian but obviously one without an ounce of emotional intelligence.

Yesterday, a hairdresser came to the house and cut most everyone's hair, including the children. Now, all the women feel especially gorgeous and the children properly shorn.

Today we are having an Easter Egg painting party. Olesya's (the chess master) family dyed the eggs; some in onion skins. The Ukrainians know their way around eggs at Easter as they are known around the globe for painting some of the most beautiful and decorative.

Jordan (my nephew) and I will contribute our traditional family plate of delicious devilled eggs.

Where will they take things when they feel so much?

Prayer, silence, faith, hope, stillness, awe: 'Know that I am God'. Psalm 46:10

78

My favourite day during Holy Week is on Saturday. It is the day following the lighting of the candles on Shabbat and the day I imagine that Mary Magdalene, Mary, mother of Jesus, Mary Clopas, Mary, mother of James, and Salome would have kept close, spending their time together grieving. In prayer, no doubt. In periods of silence, alone with the memory of their beloved.

Hope would come later for them, but not on the day of grieving. Not on a day of loss. Here at Sichów, one never knows from moment to moment what the next loss will be. The contacts back home are active and their information direct.

We are all connected in the tapestry of human compassion. Fifty-two days ago, we were complete strangers. Today, we live side by side. We eat together, sleep in the same building together, we cook in the kitchen together, we walk outside together, we grieve together.

Next Sunday is when the Ukrainians celebrate Easter. Paul has found a Polish Orthodox church in Kielce. It was very important that it not be Russian.

To tell you the truth, I don't know what hope really means. My life has been fairly privileged. There has only been once in my life that I was called to bring the word hope into question and that was when I almost lost my own son. Curiously, it didn't manifest as hope; rather, as acceptance. Like in the Serenity Prayer 'to accept the things I cannot change'. For me, this is what it means to go inside and do the spade work.

April 20, 2022
Day 56

"If Only I Could See."

> *If only I could see*
> *My fields and steppes again.*
> *Won't the good Lord let me,*
> *In my old age,*
> *Be free?*
> *I'd go to Ukraine,*
> *I'd go back home.*
> *There they'd greet me–*
> *Glad to see the old man.*
> *There I'd rest,*
> *I'd pray to God,*
> *There I'd–but why go on?*
> *There will be nothing.*
> *How am I to live in slavery*
> *With no hope?*
> *Do tell me,*
> *Please,*
> *Lest I go crazy.*
> Taras Shevchenko,
> 1848

Paul and I visited Lviv about four years ago. We went on a pilgrimage to see the frescos of Jan Rosen at the Armenian Cathedral of the Assumption of Mary and to stay at the George Hotel where Rose and Henry Kieniewicz spent their honeymoon, as well where Teresa Rostworowska's parents were married.*

The monument to Taras Shevchenko was within walking distance. I remember seeing it and have some recollection of pausing before it, curious to know who it was but not curious enough to ask.

Shevchenko was a revolutionary, a Ukrainian Icon. Not the kind that carried a gun, but the kind that wrote poetry, painted, dreamed of another kind of world and threatened Imperial Russia with his thoughts and words.

He was born into Serfdom, orphaned at eleven but was liberated from the bondage of slavery by a series of events; chiefly, the recognition that he had a rare talent for drawing at such a young age. Later, his poetry took notice.

One of his early poems insulted Czar Nicholas I so badly that he was arrested and sent on a forced march to the Ural Mountains. In exile, he was forbidden to draw, paint or write. Czar Nicholas I took pleasure in confirming his sentence by personally signing it. In the official report, Shevchenko was accused of using the 'Little-Russian language.' (Ukrainian).

"The Dream"

> *To every man his destiny,*
> *His path before him lies,*
> *One man builds, one pulls to ruins,*
> *One, with greedy eyes,*
> *Looks far out, past the horizon,*
> *Whether there remains*
> *Some country he can seize and bear*
> *With him to his grave;*
> *That one of his own kinsman robs*
> *By card-play in his home,*
> *One, crouching in the corner, whets*
> *His knife against his own*

Brother, and that one, quiet and sober,
Pious and God-fearing,
Would creep up like a kitten, wait
Until the time you're having
Some trouble, and then drive his claws
Deep into your liver–
Useless to implore–for neither
Wife nor babes will move him.

This is only the beginning of an epic poem he wrote in 1844 called "The Dream," but the similarities to today are indisputable. Striking. Especially troubling, almost foreboding is the last line written here: *Wife nor babes will move him.* (When I think that of the 10 million refugees who have fled the Ukraine, that 90% are women and children, this last line is particularly chilling).

Most of our residents left for Krakow at 6:30 this morning, hoping to be first in line when the consulate doors open. Each one needs some form or other, essential to determining their specific status. Our reliable, but often cranky bus driver, Pan T. was here early to help load the 30 who were going.

This has given me an excellent opportunity to let you know what's developing here at Sichów.

We had an Easter Egg Painting Party on Saturday. Both the children and adults participated in painting the eggs. We served sandwiches, devilled eggs, chips and sodas. Each child was given an Easter basket with chocolates and small toys.

Afterwards, we sat around the table with one of our distinguished Ukrainian families; the family of Olesya and Masha, the painters, filmmakers, illustrators. Because Paul speaks Russian, Jordan and I were able to keep up with the conversation reasonably well, as we talked about playwrights, poets, films, and finally, Russia. Oddly enough, the name of Taras Shevchenko was never mentioned, perhaps because they thought we wouldn't have known about him and, indeed, they were right. But we talked about Tchaikovsky who is from the Ukraine and we talked about Chekov and The Cherry Orchard and how the cherry orchard is actually in the Ukraine and we talked about how the Russians have, for generations, restricted the Ukrainian language by forbidding it to be spoken or ridiculing it as an inferior form of speech. It was one of those evenings where one is so absorbed with the conversation that our hardships were forgotten for those few hours.

For that brief period of time, we were not thinking about war or re-settlement, passports, money, lost family and friends, missing pets. We were there together, completely engaged.

Out of this evening, came a strong desire to create a community of artisans, craftsmen and painters. What would that look like? I was tired of second guessing the war. I don't know why I had this ridiculous idea that I wouldn't feel as jumpy when the war changed its front and focus. 'It's moving further and further East', I said to myself. But of course I didn't feel better, not one bit so. I was so anxious yesterday that I could hardly quiet myself even when lying down. When I ran into Paul's cousin at the grocery store, I burst into tears. So it is. It's like that sometimes.

I mentioned my idea, however, to Jordan and he had a better idea. (I'm delighted to have him here with us. He's a hard working guy and he's willing to jump in with any task we have going on). He felt it wasn't a good idea to create an atmosphere of expectation where the residents would feel pressure to 'move on.' I become very unpleasant myself when people tell me I should get over something or curb my emotions so I understood immediately what Jordan was saying. His idea was to simply fix up one of the rooms in the ruin as an atelier for our resident artists to have a place to go to during the day. That's it. So simple. As he explained it, 'For things to be as close to the way they were when they left the Ukraine.' And not to make anyone think that we're doing this especially for them as this can cause a sense of obligation.

We also have two or three women seamstresses and one whom I know enjoys knitting. We're thinking about buying some sewing machines and yarn and setting those up in the Orangerie.

Small steps. Simple. Welcoming.

*Last week I realised that I mentioned Marek Rostworowski and only a few of you know whom I'm talking about. Marek R. was the Minister of Culture in Poland after the War and Paul's mother's first cousin.

Teresa Horodynska Rostworowska married Jan R., Marek's brother. Her parents were married at the George Hotel. Paul's parents spent their honeymoon there in 1939.

April 25, 2022
Day 61

I met Igir in the kitchen this morning, busily making a pot of coffee for everyone, breakfast for Daria, cereal for himself, and couldn't help but notice as he skipped into place at each point of duty, how vibrant he seemed. 'Pani Amber I have the most exciting news I have heard from my parents and they are safe after a very dangerous road,' he burst out suddenly with news that came through all in one breath. I gave him such a hug which he cheerfully accepted.

Igir's parents were able to escape from a town near Kharkiv in occupied Ukraine.* They are in their early sixties, in good health and Igir is their only child. The road they had to travel was mined on either side with undetonated bombs placed there by the Russian Army. It's the width of the vehicle that decides whether you die or break out. A car, for example will have more of a chance at this than a bus or military transportation. This is designed to keep civilians in and humanitarian aid out.

He said he was on the phone with them throughout yesterday. He was radiant. His parents made it back to their apartment which has not suffered much damage and his mother was of two minds about coming to Poland. 'What about our things?' she asked. 'We'll buy new things,' he reassured. 'Mama', he consoled her, 'We have each other, our lives. We have to begin again and remember that the most important thing is each other, our lives.' He says this a lot: 'Our lives.'

'I told her this, Pani Amber, and she agreed. She said okay, they will come.'

The car is in Daria's name so they can't cross through Russian territory into Lithuania; they must come by way of another border, in this case, Poland.

Igir was beside himself with joy. And that was even before I revealed we had one more room available: Room 7. It's small but has a double bed, a private shower and a lovely view.

To see the upsurge in his excitement was quite something to behold. It's a day of noticing how the human spirit can overcome its obstacles.

We are looking at renting a small house here in the village for an overflow of residents. We are creating an artist's studio for those who express themselves in this way. We are providing two sewing machines for others who are professional seamstresses. One of our mothers makes wedding dresses.

Yes to weddings, painting, drawing, dancing, writing plays, reading poetry, making movies, studying Polish, yes to this, yes to the human spirit which will not be defeated by the scourge of war.

April 30, 2022
Day 66

> We have always had wars and personal catastrophes.
> I have no more personal fear much about that, I mean
> at my age ... but the beauty of all the life, to think that
> the billions and billions of years of evolution to build
> up the plants and the animals and the whole beauty
> of nature and that man would go and out of sheer
> shadow foolishness destroy it all and that all life would
> go from the planet and we don't know...I think it's so
> abominable ... I try to pray that it may not happen...a
> miracle happens ... I think one shouldn't give up. If you
> think of 'Answer to Job'... if man would wrestle with
> God, if man would tell God that He shouldn't do it ...
> if we would reflect more. Jung never thought that we
> might do better than just possibly sneak around the
> corner with not too big a catastrophe. When I saw
> him last, he had also a vision while I was with him
> that there he said I see enormous stretches, devastated
> enormous stretches of the earth ... but thank God it's
> not the whole planet. I think that if not more people
> try to reflect and take back their projections and take
> the opposites within themselves, there will be a total
> destruction.' Marie Louise Von Franz from 'Take Back
> The Opposites Interview.'

It's Saturday and in every respect that's what it feels
like. Altogether, if I close my eyes, I'm five again living
on North Boulevard when Mr. 'Willie' came to mow
the yard and Beulah Mae was in the kitchen, making
her legendary breads and lemon meringue pies which
perfumed the house, right up to the third floor attic.
The sun shone differently this day. The smells from the

kitchen mixed with the honeysuckle in bloom meant it was springtime in Houston on a Saturday. If I close my eyes, I am five. My life has yet to unfold and I am caught up only in the smells and the sounds around me. And now a new one has emerged. Someone must be ironing. I can smell the starch as it fuses with the steam to make a stiff press of my father's work shirts. I think of nothing but what I can hear and smell and perhaps later a trip to the five and dime store or an ice cream at the soda fountain. These are the boundaries of my world at five.

Saturdays and the sound of the lawn mower will likely always take me back to North Boulevard, to this time of being five.

As it does today, in Sichów. The weed whip is in full commission and Zoia is ironing in the library. The children are playing inside and out. Jordan is drawing. Andrei is looking at books. The water has been cut off for goodness knows what reason and we're awaiting our special visitors tomorrow; four women who escaped Mariupol. They were caught by the Russians, taken to the Urals, escaped again and made their way to Poland through Belarus.

The boundaries of our world at Sichów. One could hardly imagine that a war rages, a war within driving distance. Within this reach, women are being raped and other beastly crimes committed. There are strangers in my house.

I woke up this morning with a start as one does when one temporarily forgets the day before. I was thinking about morning-after pills being sent to the Ukraine. It's rather extraordinary that we send them automatically, like we do the weapons. Everything is distributed in such a pragmatic and rational way.

Here's a box of pills for the ladies raped, here's a box of bullets for the soldiers. If I had a poet's skill, I'd take the time to consider this aberration. The single heart cannot hold or contain these acts of violence . It has to set them outside of itself. I've often imagined, if all the single hearts in the world sent a text to each other, and made a date to show up at the border, the one within driving distance, and all these single hearts, millions of them joined together, arm in arm, forming a human shield and stormed the war, would they be bigger than the bullets? Would they be able to overtake these crimes against humanity? The women being raped? I had never thought about Rose Kieniewicz in the middle of the countryside with Russian soldiers to one side and Germans on the other, not in the light of possibly being raped, which she wasn't. That it had never occurred to me points to my naivete. Basia R. reminds me that her mother was not raped either though she would have been an easy target in the fields of Siberia. There were no toilets so one had to just relieve oneself in the open.

This is one side to the day but then there is the other. The macrocosm has its microcosm. There is the war and its horror, its destruction and monstrosities, but there is also the human imagination. There is creativity to reflect. There is a way, another way. Jordan reminds me that I miss the race when I'm thinking too much.

The art studio is now its own organism of action. It is only a question of waiting for the first boxes of art supplies to arrive. They are being donated from a former art teacher in Kentucky. We will ask for a suitable flooring to be donated and build a few shelves for storage, add a wash basin, a few drop cloths and we're on our way to making art at Sichów. We will teach classes to the children, engage them in activities of drawing, painting, working with clay and paper cut-outs.

Strangers in my house. What do I mean? Those in exile here should be at home. In a world where we do our psychological work, these talented, creative, imaginative, hard-working people would have remained strangers to me. Passers by. I might have seen one or two of our residents in Lviv a few years ago. I might have crossed in front of them on the road or sat next to them at the opera, or brushed against them in the marketplace. When strangers become intimate, it is a colorful and painful destiny. We have to carry each other even if from time to time we irritate one another.

There is no high highfalutin talk around here about highhanded morals or fireside chats about the meaning of God. The atmosphere is more one of disquietude mixed with cordiality and hard work. Everyone carries their measure of bitterness and hope.

Personally, I would like to live in a world where raping women during war is not regarded as business as usual. The first war I watched was the one my brother was in: The Vietnam War. It was the first televised war and the thirty minutes of nightly air time it received was nearly impossible to bear. There was a great disconnection within the psyche as I couldn't associate what I saw in these images with my brother, where he was and what was happening to him. Was he running for his life like those soldiers on the TV? Was he hurt? Was he frightened? Could he actually be killed? How did this work? The only thing I could understand was to protest. I didn't know what else to do, so when I was suspended from school for three days for joining the march against the war, I felt as if I had somehow joined him, I had participated in this war with him. I too had suffered a consequence. It was the connective tissue that held us together, at least in my mind.

I am not dreaming too far into the future. I am keeping close to the hour but I am imagining the easels in the studio, the smell of paint, the sound of the water as it rinses the brushes at the days end, and the lawn mower roar on Saturdays.

Soon, the world may grow tired of this war and its victims. It may move on to the next global crises. But here at Sichów, while we may grow tired, we must wrestle with God, wrestle with ourselves, we must abide by each other daily and perhaps, if inclined, continue to hope.

Tonight, before I go to sleep, I must remember to tell God that he shouldn't do it.

I'm sure those of you who read the news on a regular basis probably know that these occupied towns are displaying Russian flags, using Russian currency with Russian civil servants in place.

Another upsetting fact in this war that rages on: Rectors from the most famous Russian Universities signed a document approving the attack on the Ukraine. Not to mention the complicity of the Russian Orthodox Church. Do you see how the words, leadership, Christian, teacher, judge, church, school, has degenerated such that it carries almost no impact; these words have a detached, insincere and hollow sound. The meaning of these words are eroding from the inside out.

Upon what foundation do we expect our children to stand?

May 5, 2022
Day 71

An Open Thank You Letter To All of Our Donors

Dear Donors,
The art studio is taking shape. The Orangerie is a large, open area which sits in the cold near year-round. It opens its doors to our short summer for a few scheduled events and then patiently waits its return the following season. It will not take much to convert into a space of creativity. Tomorrow, we are driving to Krakow to buy easels and paint and paper; brushes, pencils and pens. The criterion at Sichów is: "First, Use What You Have." We have tables and chairs in house. We have a water source to include a wash basin for clean-up. We have natural lighting and french doors that lead to the park on three sides. (It seems too that we have a few artists in-house and certainly many children who want to join in on the fun.)

We are picking up our sewing machine, clearing a space for it in the upstairs Czytelnia (Reading Room/ Study and Play Area) where a project already awaits. Our seamstresses are interested in making curtains and tablecloths from the fabrics I will bring home from Krakow. Paul and I are encouraging them to make the things they'd like and we can take them to market places to sell. It's a fulfilling way for them to earn money for themselves.

The contract for the apartment in Krakow is nearing a signature. The Foundation is leasing a space in town for an unsighted couple. We will also subsidise their food bill and are currently in discussion about what other kind of support they might need for a less difficult transition.

The house is full. We are now over forty residents. Thus far we have been able to provide food, shelter, medicine, shoes, clothes, personal hygiene products, and field trips every two to three weeks. (I believe everyone is signed up to go to Tokarnia on Sunday, an ethnographic outdoor museum. It's a children's paradise).

For the forty individuals here at Sichów, it is the donors who have made the difference in their lives. Forty people. Each with a complicated, some even more complicated history/story and hardship they must daily maneuver. Sichów offers a safe and secure place from the utter confusion of the outside world. Here, children can run and play freely without fear of any harm coming to them. This alone comforts our mothers. Everyone shares in a nutritious diet, peaceful surroundings, and on Friday night's we have wine together and sometimes the women sing Ukrainian songs. It's a lively atmosphere of hard work during the week, school, and chores, and is as close to a normal life as the one left behind.

This is because of our donors. We could not have done this without you, so please accept my heartfelt gratitude for the difference you have made in the lives of those who are suffering the great loss of displacement.

Finally, I know that some of you have read our website but for those of you who have not, I would like to close with the only diary entry I have of my mother-in-law during the Ruszcza years of 1939-1945 when her manor home was filled to capacity with those seeking shelter from the war.

From her diary: A. Organization. Get up early. Indicate what work needs to be done. The cleaning, all corners of the house. B. Dedicate a specific hour in which everything in the larder is passed out. Give money to the ones who need it. C. Let all know the day before what duties will need doing the day after. D. Don't put out so much sugar when serving tea. Think about everything you do beforehand. Careful not to waste food. E. Take care of the furniture and be sure it doesn't fall into disrepair. The things that are broken, put in another place so they can be mended. F. Clean windows, beat rugs, wash linen, pack winter coats in moth balls, polish the door handles. Put everything on the calendar. G. Consider the relationships of the poor and the other house guests, take to heart their destiny. Don't ask ordinary questions. Ask myself if I have done everything for them. Look for Jesus in them and believe that Jesus is in me and will do something through me. Listen to them with great attention. Try to console them. Don't say superficial things to them but with the real love which you have within you, enter into work alongside them and make an effort to make it easier.

Rose Kieniewicz was somewhere between 19 and 24 when she wrote this. She continues to inspire me beyond the grave and that I can even attempt to the care she brought to another person's life, or even half aspire to be of service to humanity as she was, to walk a bit in these footsteps gives me profound joy. She is my north star and when there is conflict, as there is from time to time, I do find myself wondering how this young girl would have handled things.

Thank you again and I will be sending pictures of the art studio as it takes shape and of what the women decide to stitch.

God Bless You, all who have done more than their part to make someone else's life a little bit easier.

With love and my final thoughts on poets and poetry – it keeps me going.

Amber

"Poetry has the capacity to remind us of something we are forbidden to see."
Adrienne Rich.

May 12, 2022
Day 78

> I would like to ask a question which may lead us
> to something: what will make man change, deeply,
> fundamentally, radically? He has had crisis after
> crisis, he has had a great many shocks, he has been
> through every kind of misfortune, every kind of war,
> personal sorrow and so on ... If one is concerned,
> as one must be, with humanity, with all the things
> that are going on, what would be the right action
> to move man out of one direction to another ...' J.
> Krishnamurti ("Ending of Time" with Dr. David
> Bohm, 1985)

Ala is leaving next week to join her family, already in
the U.K.

I sat down yesterday, engaged my translator and said,
'I will miss you and Lady Lola.* I'm sorry you have to
leave. I want to draw a circle around us until you can
go home again.'

She responded with tears in her eyes. 'Let me tell you
about war. I have lived through two, lost two houses,
two jobs and my friends.'

What followed were more tears and talk of her travels
to London with Lola; the anticipation of reuniting with
her children again, her mother; our plan to see each
other once more, someday soon, maybe.

The war or the euphemism for war, the invasion, has
only been active for 78 days and there is a noticeable
resentment when the subject arises; an observable
inconvenience.

Today, one of the ladies who work here and has
worked here for five years, decided to call me downstairs

because she had something important to tell me. She was cleaning out the refrigerator on the right (the one least used) and felt the urge to point out the waste. She produced three small bowls and one small pot of spaghetti noodles. 'Hmm. Well? What's this, as she shakes the pot of pasta at me. 'Well?'

Hardly the quantity of waste one would expect from all meals, from seven days, from forty people, in fact, waste in these pitifully small bowls of someone's forgotten leftovers and one pot of noodles. There is no doubt of the animosity in the atmosphere, a stir beneath the surface like a geyser about to spew. It's not always evident. Sometimes it's quite subtle, like the close scrutiny from those in the grocery store, usually the ones in line behind us, the ones having to wait.

There are also the political disputes, in which I choose not to participate for a multitude of reasons, but the arguments for and against aid to the Ukrainians which those who are opposed are likely annoyed that they're having to bankroll what could be a very long war at the expense of their own needs. It's not an unreasonable grievance.

When the sun sets on Sichów, and the day's work is done, the only strength I have left is to remember that tomorrow we need to buy slippers for Natasha, medicine for Sasha, lenses for Masha, dog carriers and a suitcase for Ala, always, endlessly, the daily shopping; what we're running low on, what can we put off even until the day after tomorrow.

Then the unanswered questions that cause such an inner agitation: whose house will be destroyed next? Will anybody tell me or will I only find out in passing afterwards? Is there a friend or acquaintance left behind now buried under the rubble? Is there someone in need of greater care? Who was especially hurting today? Who is putting on the bravest face? Who is afraid to ask for something they need but don't want to trouble us? Did I remember to buy hot chocolate for Olesya and her grandfather? Have I told someone today how beautiful they look?

Not everyone is in such a situation of sensitivity so it's not surprising that there is conflict around the subject of assistance, which is probably why I try to find my peace of mind in poetry.

What will make us change, deeply, fundamentally, radically?

I don't know the answer to this question and likely never will, so the best I can do is carry on every day, even when I'm tired and don't feel like shopping for forty people, or don't feel like being nice because I might be feeling irritable or unwell and even when I'm scared about our future here, I must find my way to renewal.

Isn't that what being human is? Friendship? Remembering the other who suffers just like you, who hurts like you, who is scared like you, who is irritable and not feeling like being so nice like you? Each and every one of us here must find our way together alongside our human emotions, our disadvantages, our bad days and our good ones. We're not really all that different, one from the other. We must care for each other, remembering this, that we are more alike than we are different. For me this war is not about politics or pundits who spout their high-handed opinions. It's about clean sheets and drawing paper, sharpened pencils, blueberries in season and ice cream from time to time because it's a treat.

Grażyna Chrostowska, Polish poet died at Ravensbruck at the age of 22. She was shot in the forest alongside her sister, Apolonia. This is the poem she wrote two hours before she was executed for being a young girl who said 'no' to the Nazis.

"Anxiety"

This day is just like Chopin's "Anxiety",
The birds are low above the ground, restless,
Startled from their nests. They are listening ...
Silence in nature. Heat, like before the storm.
Low, dark clouds flow from the west.
Spring gales roll through the sky
Crouching fear in my heart. Longing, longing ...
I want to walk on soggy, distant roads,
Listen to the roar of winds, catch the breath of spring,
Feel the deepest, find the silence of love,
I go, I do not find, I change and I come back.
The cottagers were somewhere far away,
Clouds that went east,
And on the east side,
There are lonely trees, dark, inclined,
In the wind they stand and silence,
Shaken with anxiety.

This war for me is not about politics. What the hell is that anyway? It's about the human suffering all around me.

May 21, 2022
Day 87

> We understand more about fascism than we did in the 1930s. We now know where it led. We should recognize fascism, because then we know what we are dealing with. But to recognize it is not to undo it. Fascism is not a debating position, but a cult of will that emanates fiction. It is about the mystique of a man who heals the world with violence, and it will be sustained by propaganda right to the end. It can be undone only by demonstrations of the leader's weakness. The fascist leader has to be defeated, which means that those who oppose fascism have to do what is necessary to defeat him. Only then do the myths come crashing down. Dr. Timothy Snyder, Professor of History, Yale U., Opinion Guest Essay, NYT (May 19, 2022)

Hope of a return is in the hearts of many an exile. The Russians are moving further away from Kharkiv toward the Donbas region. There is still conflict, shelling and bombing within 40 km of the area from which our residents once lived, so no one is rushing to get back though longing to go home. I understand that the infrastructure is coming back to life. There is a probability that the underground transportation system will be operational again soon and schools are resuming their studies online. There are sufficient food supplies though petrol is a problem. Only 10 litres per car allowed. I don't know if that's once a week or less or more for that matter, but I do know that those who depend on their cars for work could not manage on such a small amount. The distressing news is that the Ukrainians have had to surrender Mariupol.

Depending on whom you speak and on the hour of the day, some say that there is still more to come; that in the West of the country there are random missile attacks and the Donbas is completely destroyed. Dnipro is also under attack according to those from that city.

But yesterday was Olesya's birthday! She turned seven. It was quite the celebration. Everyone received a hand-written invitation and everyone attended. There were puzzles and games and water balloons and rope swings, cake, candies and grilled meats. After the children went to bed, many of us continued to indulge in the festivities, drinking wine and talking politics. It's not my pastime, especially considering the language barrier, but I've been to enough outdoor parties in Poland to know that after all the talk winds down, there will be singing if you're patient enough to wait. I was not disappointed. Fortunately, the singing carried on into the night long after it became apparent that we can do nothing to influence the leadership of a country short of revolution. Yulia and I, with the help of a translator, concluded this revolution would look like small communities who valued the imagination, art, music, poetry and the skills required to care for oneself such as tailoring ones own clothes, growing one's own food, living off-grid, caring for each other, defending each other. Yes, I know, the high-minded idealism of a Utopia, and we know where that can lead. Still ... to wake up to the strings of the violin sounding, the poet struggling with the pen, the breeze, the children playing in harmony and the occasional conflict, does seduce one into thinking the idea of a small community might not be such a bad idea.

This is how we're managing at Sichów. There are two women who are working in the garden on a work agreement, both paid employees. We anticipate a flourishing organic garden this year, provided the rain cooperates, otherwise, we will be watering a lot.

There is the formidable Natasha in the kitchen, also a paid employee who works as hard as a team of oxen. Each family joins her on their appointed day of cooking producing the most delicious soups and salads.

Oksana Kravchenko and Oksana Kholod have transformed our tables with their beautiful table linen and are now busily making summer clothes for the children. Did I mention the curtains? I think we need to buy one more machine.

Sasha and Sasha are helping Romek in the parkland, trimming trees, clearing leaves, raking new gravel, keeping the grounds looking beautiful.

Our gardeners have also cleared a space in front of the house for cut flowers.

The students are busy with schoolwork, the pre-schoolers are adjusting to their new environment, and everyone in the house is savouring the weather to its fullest.

The Polish tutor comes twice a week to a room full of attendees and twice a week Paul instructs Olesya on the recorder. If you're lucky enough to be around when the two of them are practicing together, you won't regret it.

We are like a family, making the best of our days together under these most extraordinary circumstances. It might be worth mentioning that a few tears fell yesterday because Olesya's father missed his daughter's birthday for the first time in her 7 years.

It is also worth mentioning that the tears of the Ukrainian women are not impotent, but tears with backbone and belligerence.

"It's the saddest thing to leave home on an autumn morning where nothing forebodes a timely return ..."
~Tadeusz Różewicz, "Sobbing Superpower."

May 28, 2022
Day 94

Let me start with a short anecdote. When I worked at the Jung Centre in Houston, Jim Hollis was the director, my boss. For those of you who don't know Jim's work, I strongly encourage you to look him up and order any of his books, all of his books. You can't go wrong.

One day when I showed up for work, I was in a very bad mood much like "Alexander and the Terrible, Horrible, No Good Very Bad Day" who wants to move to Australia. In fact, I think I must have said something to that effect that I'd like to move Australia. And Jim, in his infinite wisdom said: "Just remember, wherever you go you take yourself with you."

We've had enough tears for one day. Alla left yesterday to join her family in the UK. Vlady and Lena left today amidst more tears and heaving rain, for Turkey where friends are waiting to receive them. I will miss them terribly but I'm also looking forward to hearing about their new lives elsewhere.

What I want to share today has been on my mind for a while and I'd like to set the record straight. I get the distinct impression that there are those who read these diaries who think that Sichów is a kind of Arcadia. Some kind of pastoral fairyland where all get along and work together in this harmonious bubble without discord. Well it's not. Nothing could be further from the truth.

Imagine for a moment that you happen to live in a small hotel. Then imagine that a war breaks out literally three hours from your house. Native Houstonians (my home town) think Dallas, for example. And within two weeks, your small hotel, your home, has lovingly opened itself up to forty strangers in need of a place to shelter. The end. Well, not exactly.

We have been together now since February 28th, three months to the day. It's extraordinary that we get along as well as we do. But there are forty (including ourselves – forty-two) active realities in process at all times.

Forty-two unique individuals with their own calling, their own suffering, dreams, ailments, complexes, shadow, complaints and projections in daily motion.

Who sets the tone? Good question. Is it Paul and I or is it Sichów or what Sichów represents? Who sets the tone in a family? Obviously, that depends on the nature and personality of the family. I would have to say it's a blend of Paul and I and how we have, over the past seven years, come to define Sichów.

Forty-two personalities and their individual impulses did not change because of war; however, at the beginning, when we were all thrust together there was a momentary pause, a kind of calm before the storm. The children hardly made a sound. I was very suspicious, as this has never been the case in my experience. We were all polite, placing a slight distance between ourselves, almost afraid to cough out loud. But "... remember, wherever you go you take yourself with you."

As we have become more familiar with each other, it's nothing that we crowd shoulder to shoulder at the stove to dish out our portion and maybe some of another's onto our plate. It's nothing to us now to carve out our personal space at the tea kettle for a cup of coffee, even if that means overlapping with your neighbour also waiting for the water to boil or take the last slice of cake, or hone in on the of strawberries if you happen to be fortunate enough when they're delivered and seize a share for yourself before they disappear.

The children are doing their work too: they are noisy much of the time, often outside my door, misbehaving, fitful and all the things one expects from a child .

That's the top layer. Next in order are the misunderstandings between us which cause conflict and residual resentment if not resolved.

Not everyone who showed up that day in February came with charity in their hearts or a sense of fair play or for those who were self-centred before the war. Well ... they're still self-centred as the war rages on and will be, likely, at its end. This is how we are.

But when you're motivated by something greater than yourself, something outside of yourself that throughout the years has encouraged an inner journey to self-discovery and ultimately, to some sense of gnosis, then you are able to see with a greater clarity.

We decided to rearrange some of the women's duties. The kitchen had turned into a toxic cauldron. One woman took on the role of a manager, started to boss the volunteers, control the supplies in a way that made others want to run away. My husband will be displeased if I say what I'm really thinking, as he reminds me to forgive 7 times 70 a day. He notices the acacia in bloom. He takes greater pity upon others when all I see is a Pitbull heading my way and my first line of defence is to protect myself.

But it does come down to toxicity. And even he would agree. The last thing we can afford right now is for any one of us to misappropriate the space for either our own personal gain or our own unconscious, unnoticed core complexes which are being constantly triggered.

I can, to a point, tolerate unconscious behaviour until it becomes so active that it disrupts the whole, the collective. And then, we will rearrange things.

I have reclaimed the kitchen and we're back to what we had before our disturbance, which is families sign up to cook for everyone, one day a week, without supervision. Women cooking for their families don't need to be micromanaged.

There are other personality traits that really goad me like the idea of entitlement when Paul and I are working every angle to make sure our donations see us through the fall. So for someone to ask for something personal, apart from basic needs, when the rest of us have to share causes an explosion inside me. And when I say basic needs, I make sure everyone has an appointment with the hair dresser. I make sure there are clothes and shoes and medicine and nutritious foods available and always, always, cake. (We need cake. Send cake).

Between us, we have one washing machine which I've used twice in the last three months. I wear the same outfit 7-10 consecutive days before I change as there are women here with children who have special needs and believe me, they need that washing machine. So when someone asks me for their own personal drying rack when we already have three, I go insane. How can they not see? Jordan helps me though. He's given me a mantra to recite: No. No. and more No. My wise nephew.

War does wound us, but it does not change us, not fundamentally at least. It might be the catalyst to encourage us to go inside and do what I call the spade work, but it's not a guarantee. This is how it is. The scars of war.

The beauty of all of this, however, is that the art studio is now active and there are artists painting in watercolours, acrylic and oils on canvas, paper and textiles. Gala is conducting art classes for the children on Saturday mornings. It's full of life and creativity.

The garden is in bloom and will produce vegetables by July. Sichów has really never looked so well, so consistently active and so full of imagination.

This atmosphere of inspiration co-exists alongside the toxicity. In a community such as ours where we are all interconnected and bound to each other until outside circumstances shift, then we have to include all of our shadows, our projections and our misunderstandings that result from being in such close proximity. We do not have the option to relocate or to ask another to leave because we might be made uncomfortable, not those who are left anyway because those who are left are only thinking of going home again.

The hope that I spoke about a week ago has waned with Russia now bombing the life out of the Donbas.

But we sat at the table last night with Andrei and his family and we all agreed that we must keep some kind of hope alive even if for only the children's sake. Especially the children. We must be their guiding light. We must be. We are a human family of hope.

Which brings me to the close of this diary noting the deaths of the children at Robb Elementary School in Uvalde, Texas.

We can no longer turn our backs on the psychological nature of man. We are at the end of the road. We must make a decision to look inside of ourselves, once and for all.

June 10, 2022
Day 107

What next?

The war is taking a turn none of us expected, especially the renewed attacks on Kyiv where explosions and a barrage of missile attacks disrupted their previous, month-long stillness. Yesterday, a grocery store in Kharkiv was bombed.

Vladysława's text from Turkey:

> Last month, I thought that probably it would be possible to come back nearest time and the situation becoming more calm, but now again it seems that 'there is not light at the end of the tunnel' and it will be continuing a long time. In Kharkiv, they are bombing every day, but in spite of this a lot of people have come back, at least now transport works and there is no humanitarian problem, so if you have money and do not lose job there, is possible to live.
>
> Big problem with Mariupol, Kherson and people lost their hope that these cities will come back to Ukraine. People already can get their Russian passport, so if some Ukrainians support 'Russian World' they can go to Kherson and officially get Russian passport.
>
> I still have hope deep inside to come back home by the end of summer, but time will show.

Vladysława was our first resident to appear at Sichów with her mother, Lena, and Daria, who was pregnant at the time. (Daria is still here, now with her daughter Diana, husband Igir, and his parents, Tatiana and Sasha.) If Vladysława cannot go back home, she and her mother will likely return to Sichów.

Clearly, however, if they are bombing grocery stores in Kharkiv, it makes sense that they are trying to create a humanitarian crisis, much like what they did in Mariupol.

What next?

Natalia is our precious five-year-old with Down Syndrome, Autism, heart condition and now a hernia that needs surgery. Paul has uncovered every stone trying to get this surgery pushed through the NFZ (our national health provider) without much success. The several cardiologists with whom he has consulted say that there has to be another complete set of tests before they will consider surgery, plus we must wait another year. These tests were run in the Ukraine just before the war, so Paul drove them an hour away to a translator of medical documents hoping translated tests will be accepted. Presumably, there is a law in Poland that allows for only Polish doctors to conduct such tests when considering further surgeries. She is a plucky little creature, but, still, having had two previous open-heart surgeries, the thought of now another operation requiring general aesthesia is a reason to proceed cautiously which may mean going private. Once the tests from the Ukraine are translated, then we can take the next step in searching for another cardiologist who can see us within a reasonable time frame and can advise to our legal restrictions (if there really are any) and, basically, direct us to the safest, most expedient path possible.

In the kitchen this week, we've had two groups of women cooking. One group preparing lunch for the community and the other preparing meals for artists in the Palace. (A commitment we made two years ago to host artists from America.)

There were about eight of us in the kitchen circumventing potential collision yesterday as we maneuvered our way to the finish line. What made it all the more interesting is that one group was preparing vegan dishes while the other the usual Ukrainian fare, I'd say encountering more than a physical collision but a culinary ideology as one cook looked suspiciously at the other.

The artists in the Palace are working on a project pioneered by a woman in New York whose Polish/Jewish grandmother miraculously survived the Holocaust. She works with maps, showing how there were high-functioning Jewish villages before the war (including schools, synagogues, bakers, tailors, butchers) and then how the demographic changed considerably after the war. It's a fascinating project which has expanded over the years to includes memoir writing and music. The central theme of the work is: loss.

Our residents don't know about this project even though the visiting artists were eager to hear their stories of loss, Paul and I declined on their behalf. There was even a suggestion of reframing the question of what a future home or a rebuilding of a destroyed one would look like. In either case, the sensitivity is notable. As written in Ecclesiastes, "To everything there is a season ... a time to keep silence and a time to speak ..." It is too soon to speak of loss because no one knows to what extent the loss. The war is not over.

One of the hardest concepts to communicate to someone is active war. Not even I entirely understand.

As I gaze out my window on our trees in full leaf, the sun casting its shadows, the children at play creating a picture of beauty and serenity, how can I imagine a scorched landscape with plumes of smoke rising on the horizon? And yet, it was like this here in Poland eighty years ago.

There is a time for action and a time for reflection. What happened in Poland during WWII can now be reflected upon. We can write books and films and plays and make art and paint and dance this story, but not for the Ukrainians, not now.

Now the women must cook. They must garden. They must sew. They must paint beautiful landscapes. They must read playful, happy stories to their children. They must take the bus to town. They must gather on Friday nights to drink wine together and tell their own stories to each other, not the ones we may want to hear as a spectator. This is a private world exclusive to those who understand the concept of active war.

What next?

Igir, Dasha and baby Diana are moving are moving to Krakow in the morning. I stepped away a few moments ago to get a cup of coffee and met Igir in the kitchen who told me the news. His company has opened an office in Krakow. I knew the move was imminent, but I didn't know how much trouble they'd had over the past month – the failed attempts to secure an apartment after they'd been promised one, having to be in constant contact with social media watching for opportunities which would be listed and then ten minutes later, removed. He told me that he was once fifteen miles from the city centre on his way to sign a lease on an apartment unseen when the landlord said, sorry, not available anymore. In addition, Dasha said that her parents live very near where the grocery store in Kharkiv was bombed yesterday or the day before but they don't want to leave just yet. They keep hoping but Dasha says that already the rouble is becoming currency in many parts of the Ukraine, specifically near to where her parents live, and she so wishes they would join them in Krakow. As it is, the apartment there is far too small for four adults and a baby but they must start over again somewhere. Dasha agreed with me that the Russians will continue to bomb the Ukraine's food supplies.

The other crisis about to develop in Poland is from areas like Zakopane where hotels have been accommodating refugees but are now asking all to leave unless they can pay. We have a family here with other family members in a hotel and they've been asked to leave. When they were offered Sichów, they declined saying they would seek help from the volunteer service near them to find them accommodation. I hope they find something because we have a mother, grandmother and baby coming across the border in a few days for the room where Igir and Dasha were staying.

What next? What's on my mind?

I am worried about the Ukrainians in winter with no heat and food supplies in short order. I am worried about the refugees here in Poland without adequate care. I worry about the children with special needs and the animals left behind.

Two days ago, one of the women came up to me in a slight panic. Her son had torn his shoes. They were ruined and he only had this one pair. How would he go to school? It was 6:30 in the evening and I was already quite tired but there was something so tangible in her voice, in her eyes: Her boy had no shoes. There is something archetypal about shoes and I couldn't explain it to Paul who wanted me to wait until the next day to go out but I insisted on taking them at that moment. The relief was immediate. I've been to holocaust museums throughout Europe and in America and there is something about the shoes that I can't explain but it sends me into a state of despair when I think of someone who hasn't a pair of shoes. We bought two pairs for him and two for mama. They didn't want to take advantage so they didn't mention they had only the shoes they came with when they crossed the border.

And finally, dear Paul who keeps up with all the doctor's appointments taking this one here and that one there, acting translator and comforter for those who are sick and frightened in a foreign country.

I have much more to say but it must wait until the next instalment.

'Till then. Thank you for reading, thank you for caring, thank you for your contributions. I perish to think where we'd be without you.

Paul and Olesya, Recorder Lesson

Cross Border House. Drawing by Olesya

Ukrainian Trident

Olesya and Sasha playing chess

Group Photograph

From left to right: Zoia, Gala, Masha, Iryna, Olesya, Luba, Oksana, Jordan, Stefan, Andrei, Yevgenia, Jana, Marina, Danilo, Paulina, Melanie holding Natalia, Oksana holding Volo, Stepan, (crouching), Nadia, Igir, Masha, Betsy, Amber

Paul with Recorder

The Wonder of Jana

Paul and Volo (Happy Town)

Nadia and Natalia

Olesya and Delikates

Jordan and Natalia, Art Project

Volo Juumping

Amber and Children, Christmas

Rehearsing at Kurozwęki

Marina's Birthday

Gala and Jordan

Gala and Children, Christmas

Olesya, Halloween

Jordan, Volo, and Svietek

Margo, Misha and Bogdan

Saying Goodbye

Left to right: Gala, Andrei, Zoia, Olesya, Masha, Oksana, Paul, Iryna, Oksana, Luba, Marina, Natasha, Oksana, Viktoria, Stepan, Olga, Yulia

June 18, 2022
Day 115

In 1998, I had the great privilege of hearing Dr Edward Said lecture at Rice University in Houston, Texas. He spoke to us about his philosophy, his life and his music. In particular, what comes to mind this morning is his book, *Out of Place: A Memoir.*

Anouar Antara in his article on Said and Exile writes, as predictable, his first days in the USA were tough and he describes his arrival in the American continent as the saddest day in his life. In addition, the author himself has recorded in his writings that his own life experience was always conditioned by the circumstance of displacement and alienation with respect to his birth place. In this regard, he states the following in his above-mentioned memoir:

> Along with the language, it is geography –
> especially in the displaced form of departures,
> arrivals, farewells, exile, nostalgia homesickness,
> belonging, and travel itself – that is the core of
> my memories of those early years. Each of the
> places I lived in – Jerusalem, Cairo, Lebanon,
> the United States – has a complicated, dense
> web of valences that was very much part of
> growing up, gaining an identity, forming my
> consciousness of myself and of others. (Said,
> 2000: Prefix p xii.)

What does it mean to be an exile? I frequently ask myself this question.

After three partitions, in 1772, Poland lost much of its land to Prussia, Russia and Austria. In 1793, a bit more, until in 1795, Poland was no longer a country, but a traveling group of nomads looking for a charitable situation in other countries. Intrinsic to any culture is its language and this is how the Polish people identified themselves over the next two hundred years. They never stopped speaking their language, even when forbidden by the Czar; such as was the case for the Kieniewicz's (Paul's grandparents) in Belorussia or White Russia, now known as Belarus. They practiced their religion when able. They sang their native songs and prepared the food of their ancestors.

My mother-in-law, Rose Popiel, unlike her husband, Henry Kieniewicz, was born into new Poland, a country with borders. It wasn't to last but for twenty years it was there, before it once again disappeared, this time to war, then to occupation.

When Rose and Henry crossed into Scotland with nothing but the clothes on their backs and the shoes on their feet, they arrived in Bankfoot, a small community about 8 miles north of Perth. They knew no one except other exiles from a defunct Polish army, now known as combatants (a mix of officers and lower ranking soldiers). The living conditions for this young couple were deeply dissatisfying. Rose told me that she couldn't keep Theresa from crying and the landlady was prickly to say the least. This young woman had come through a war, cared for refugees, defied the occupying communists by distributing her furnishings, silver, paintings and other family valuables throughout Kraków, I might add, illegally transporting them by night, but was beside herself in Scotland with an overbearing landlady who insisted on keeping a crying baby quiet. So when Henry made an alliance with the Earl of Scone Palace to care for the grounds and start a market garden of his own, the stone cottage in Old Scone provided to them opened up like a castle for Rose. With no indoor plumbing and no heat other than that of a paraffin stove, she recounts her sense of jubilation that she now had her own home. Her privacy was once again restored. Her babies could fit and cry in freedom.

Sometimes I get the distinct impression that there is a prejudice against those in exile, otherwise known as outcasts, expatriates, displaced persons, persona non grata, or, simply, refugees. I realise I have referenced this subject before, but it bears repeating to the raised eyebrow of one who questions how the exile should live. I do encounter some visitors to Sichów who are surprised by the high functioning level of activity here and at times, sense in their surprise, a measure of subtle reproach.

So, here is the question. Why should people, classified as refugees, be so fortunate as to have access to an art studio in which to paint, draw or craft or a sewing machine endowed with good quality fabrics on which to make clothes or other items of choice? Is this a luxury reserved only for those in a settled political situation?

Why should they be treated to soft fruits such as strawberries, served with cream and sugar when they are in a position of charity. Are not these amenities reserved only for those who work hard, pay taxes, those of whom are in a stable and established circumstance, those who can afford such things? Is it even our ethical responsibility to allow a foreigner such a delicacy, or is it good enough to simply supply bread, water, cheese, some meat and a bed? Does it not provoke resentment from others, such as the local population who see this level of charity? Should not the foreigner instead accept their station in a reduced class, an uninvited guest, and submit to a lower wage-earning status of field and housework?

I do not find these questions complicated because I literally believe that all the residents living here today are equal to me and I to them. Nothing separates us but history, place and personal interests.

Henry met Rose when he went to work as an estate manager for her father, where they lived in a manor house much like Sichów. In fact, it's been told that he even came here to Sichów in his young years to improve his skills by observing Krzysztof Radziwiłł. When Rose and Henry married, the dowry gifted them was the manor house near Kraków called Ruszcza. I am certain they had no doubt of their future plans to carry on the family traditions of land ownership and the responsibilities that came with it.

Quoting Rose: "If anyone told me that by the time I was twenty-five I'd be living in Scotland, I would have said they were from the moon."

Henry was a perfect match for his bride. He was educated, intelligent, well spoken, well read, and I've been told by his children he had a quirky sense of humour and a kind heart. He was a religious man. A good man. None of these things changed because of war. He did not stop being religious nor did he lose his ability to think critically, to laugh, to read, to express compassion nor did he compromise his integrity.

Of course there are those living here who did not live in a manor house in the Ukraine before the war. It's most probable that some lived paycheck to paycheck without the possibility of consistently affording strawberries in cream with sugar. There are also those who appreciated a different kind of lifestyle. Artists, filmmakers, musicians and wedding dress makers.

There are the well travelled Ukrainians here and those who never left their borders.

The philosophy behind the Sichów model of sheltering and rebuilding depends on a few key points. The defining of the words charity, dignity, and psychology are integral to the way Paul and I conduct ourselves and the decisions we make.

I don't feel like a charity though we are charitable in the sense that we are broad minded in our thinking. However, I don't feel anyone here, and I'm confident I can speak for Paul, is in any way inferior to us. Charity from the lopsided paradigm of: "I have and you don't" breeds contempt.

Sociologists have confirmed the backlash from 'charity' bestowed upon those who are perceived poor by those who are rich and think they are helping but in fact are resented for what seems to be instead an appearance of rescuing and infantilising. Rose's daughter, Mary, has worked as a missionary in South America for forty-five years. She literally serves the poor. Not in an obliging way, but in an authentic, Christ-like way, living there together with the poor. She herself has taken up the mantle of poor. Before I met her, Rose said, "My daughter, Mary, wears the face of poverty.

Our philosophy is based on sustainability and self-sufficiency; living together. Yes, the Foundation provides the monetary means to create such an environment and for this we are eternally grateful to our donors.

But the art studio is here to maintain dignity. So is the sewing centre. Some have already lost their homes, some fear they will be the next but all share in the loss of a country, at least for the moment. All are out of place. All are victims of war.

Unfortunately, we live in a world now of collective psychosis and there are some very precious children here who should be fiercely protected. One of the ways we protect is to provide. Sichów is a child's garden of verse and play. In the art studio are drawing and painting classes and in the library room upstairs are books, puzzles, games and toys. (And as I've said before, if you're lucky enough to be here on Tuesdays and Fridays you can listen in on Paul giving Olesya a recorder lesson. Magic.) The healthy psychology of a community is based on the health of the individual. If the residents here are at moderate peace and if Sichów can lessen their anxieties, then we stand a good chance at maintaining a community in balance.

My husband's family never truly integrated into the British culture. This is not to say they didn't have a good life there, only to say that it's unnatural to be aborted from ones culture of origin by force. It's usually without preparation that one finds oneself in such a position.

Once I got to know the Kieniewicz's and their background, their history, I was speechless that these people of such dignity and character were misunderstood and treated like servants, worse yet, like bad children or idiots. Of course this attitude didn't carry on throughout their lives in the UK but to say there was an ultimate integration would be inaccurate. I think unless you married into the family, it would be difficult to understand the scope to which they suffered loss. And the scope to which they had to rebuild through learning a new language, a new cuisine, habits, mannerisms, humour, music, dance, art, all of these things which are part of a culture that now you, as the orphan child, must adopt.

No war is any different from any other war in this sense. All war produces this displacement of its citizens. All wars leave them homeless and vulnerable.

I propose to use the word support rather than charity. To partner, even better. Never lose sight of the dignity in another regardless of how you feel about them. This is not easy because they may not be demonstrating the same toward you, themselves or others. But because we live in a structured environment I believe we can practice this level of respect toward each other with a bit less difficulty.

We do not live lavishly, we live creatively. We must live creatively if we are to maintain psychological health.

Finally, I want to share a photograph of Rose and her first cousins, the Rostworowski's: Jan and Marek. This picture was taken after the war in front of the Old Scone cottage, Rose's Castle. It's the broad smile on her face that reveals to me in every sense a renewal, a victory of having come through the worst of it. She looks so at home sitting between them.

June 29, 2022
Day 126

Between the bombing of the shopping mall in Kremenchuck and the reinforcement of Nato's Readiness Action Plan, (which increases the presence of Polish and American soldiers at the border,) there is a sense of dread in the air. The mind so quickly springs into action as it plays out the worst possible scenarios which rarely happen as one imagines them; still, this is a specialty of the mind which we all must bear. That doesn't mean I ignore the signs of a protracted and bloody war, but beyond this observation, given I cannot actually plan for something of unknown origin, it's best to let the mind rest. To torture the mind with dystopian thoughts of some impending doomsday occurrence is a complete and total waste of my time. Which doesn't mean I don't feel anxious about how an attack on humanity of this scale will play out, it just means that I can't simply sit around thinking the worst. It will undo me and I can't afford to be in that position as there are too many who depend on the stability and the fortitude of a community we have built together.

What do I do? What do I think about instead? How do I best direct my thoughts so as not to deplete myself of energy before I'm even out of the shower? Some days, like today, I'm not so fortunate as to dodge all bullets, but I will get to that in a moment.

I work. I attend to the needs of our residents which are multiple and frequent. And then I try to use my thoughts creatively. I am always on the lookout for what they are teaching me. This is the way I align myself with something bigger than my petty thoughts.

I pray. Not just the begging kind, as if I'm some sort of victim and plead for all my suffering to end and all circumstances be tidied up to suit my own personal comfort, but honest prayer, in contemplation, in partnership with the mystery within me, within all of us. You can call this mystery God, Our Mother or The Divine, Adonai, The Way of the Tao, The Buddha but there must be a call, a crying out in the night for help. I cannot go far without this relationship. If I don't connect with what I know to be my life force, that which supports, nurtures, guides and informs me, then I don't stand a chance at service. It would be impossible to serve in such a challenging situation if I were not in a relationship with Christ.

I've yet to shower this morning, assuming there's even water. Last week we were without water for a full 48 hours. It was intermittent before that and with the current heat wave, is still unreliable. We did go to the lake on one of those days. We packed a picnic lunch of sandwiches, juice and fruit. Most everyone went swimming; some took a paddleboat ride, and we all had ice cream before coming home. For those few hours, we were able to forget about the war.

Let me tell you. The magic of having no water is that when it finally does come back on, there's no better shower than this. It's one way to think. Maybe it's not for everyone but it's how I move through life.

There was a recent birthday party for the woman who gets on my nerves. In the morning of that day I thought that at least I should be kind and buy her some flowers because she was already cooking for her own party, including the baking of the cake. I got the idea that if she didn't make her own party, then no one would, but in fact, most of us only celebrate with a small store-bought cake anyway, a song and some flowers. I have come to regard her behaviour as desperate. She's a difficult person to like; most of us endure her. It so happened too, that on this day, in the morning, the county called to say that there were no more Ukrainians in the area except for those here and at Kurozwęki (our neighbouring family estate). If we would like to avail ourselves of any donations lying about the fire station, then to feel free to come and have a look. Paul and I wasted no time driving over to see what was left. To my surprise, there were a few bags of clothes which I brought back to Sichów with me. Our birthday girl muscles in and starts a pile straight away. One of the women who works here wasn't aware that this was a private stack of clothes, saw a skirt on top and thought that it would look nice on one of the other ladies standing there. When our employee reached for it, my least favourite snatched it out of her hands and said it belonged to her. G. snatched it right back and held it up to the woman she believed it would fit nicely. The lady declined saying it wasn't her style. How gracious she was. (I could use a lesson or two.)

My moral dilemma set in at that moment. Why should I buy flowers for someone I don't like? I didn't want to. I didn't even want to go to her party. I lost all sense of maturity and compassion. As I went from shop to shop that day buying what we needed for the house, I passed a lot of flower stands. At the start of the day I actually considered going to the florist to buy her a hand picked, beautifully designed arrangement of flowers. What I brought home instead was a small bunch of ordinary flowers that I regarded as 'good enough'. I gave them to her and she nodded. There wasn't much exchange of friendship from either of us.

Living with so many other people under such unusual circumstances cannot help but bring out the best and the worst inside you. And after so many years of analysis, I'm not afraid of the part of me that's not so pleasant. The objective is to own it and not project it. The task is to carry it yourself. I had to continue to do what's in my nature, and it's in my nature to buy the flowers even if I don't like you very much.

I don't have any great revelatory comments to make about myself as to what I discovered that day other than I'm as human and as complicated as the next person. To not make a situation worse feels more natural to me than the decision to consciously hurt someone else. I can still be civilised even if I don't care for another person or their actions.

So today. There was the repairman whom we called, about our washing machine that ran constantly all day long and into the night. The locking mechanism on the door jammed. When Paul explained the urgency, that we have 40 plus people using it on a daily basis, he replied, "I don't care what your problem is. I still can't get there until next week." Paul was stunned but pushed on, "Yes, but some of our residents have children with special needs who depend on the washing machine on a daily basis." To which he repeated, "That's not my problem."

We bought a new machine . The old one will eventually be repaired. It will be nice to have two.

Following the impact of such caustic speech, we received a phone call from a woman who volunteers for us in an educational capacity. To our surprise, though I will be honest more to mine than to Paul's, she announces that she's been telling some of our residents they really ought to move to Canada.

This was this final blow for me today. The idea that someone who spends so little time here at Sichów and further to that, isn't qualified, should issue such a declarative. There's nothing even sensible in such a statement. The woman knows no one in Canada, as far as I know, certainly not someone who's able to take on so many and with special needs.

One might say to me that's she's just an old busybody and doesn't have enough in her life of interest, so she must stick her nose into my affairs and tell everyone here who's settling in that they should now up and move to Canada, with no plan, no job, no language nor lodging.

If the situation were not so delicate, I'd disregard her without a thought. Fortunately, after a few inquiries, the residents confessed they thought it was a very strange suggestion but kept quiet under the circumstances that she was 'helping' us. It's becoming like this: a mix of do-gooders and those who bear a grudge about the Ukrainians even being here, each camp formulating their opinions without much practical experience.

One of our donors sent an email to me recently.

"All of you at Sichów are exercising 'hospitality' in many forms and expression...same root as the word hospital. Lodging, inn, shelter. The Latin uses the same word for both guest and host. There is a beautiful spirit at Sichów – that is evident to me." ~ Karen from Canada.

It meant the world to me because with all our weaknesses and doubts, there is an ever present human spirit that runs through like a steel pipe connecting all of us. We truly are at this moment in time an active and engaged community whose ultimate interest is each other and each other's well being even if that means someone would like to relocate to Canada.

What the lady doesn't know because she doesn't live here and is not involved in community meetings and communications is that Canada is really only an option for the young if you have extended family there. Most are waiting to go home again.

> It just turned out that way. I felt that these people before this great war broke loose all around them, should end up in some place, where time had stopped and where all the fragile and brittle and useless and unnecessary things that people surround themselves with were gathered. And in the midst, of this collection of all these little things there should be this completely brittle and completely useless and terrified person. So you have the feeling that that person and all those things have reached their final moment on earth...with all these wars in which two great powers collide ... you can't help but identify with the third parties caught in the middle. I suppose that's the fear we all carry inside. ~ Ingmar Bergman, Speaking in an interview about his film, *Shame*, 1968.

July 4, 2022
Day 131

> "I give up my desire for security. I give up my desire for inordinate affection and approval. I give up my desire for power and control. There's also a saying that sums up all three but doesn't identify them (individually) ... I give up my desire to change the situation ... I think as the spiritual journey advances, there are more intense moments than the dark nights even, but they're very brief...those experiences of being emotionally thrust into a kind of pit where you can't rid of the feeling or the misery or the grief or the hatred or the resentment, the bitterness ... it's still based on a feeling however justified in itself... you have the feeling of sheer helplessness in the face of the conditions that are overwhelming ... the happy ending is to just forget about yourself (He is referencing the ego, of course, not the Self)." Fr. Thomas Keating.

I listen to Father Keating a lot these days as my faith is tested. I look for ways to practice trust. The spiritual journey is always a journey into the unknown and this fact, one must accept. To remind myself that I cannot change the circumstance of war and the suffering of others, nor can I change the mounting discontent among those who are not in exile, what I can do is give up my desire for control, which is a battle I know I cannot win.

Normally, I send out these war diaries every eight to ten days but this one comes as a response to an email I received from my friend, Marla, in Los Angeles who was planning to come to Kraków to help with the Ukrainian crisis. She learned through a friend already here that the church has taken down the tents that served as a hub for those in need of shelter and food. Her friend goes on to say that she is in an indoor shelter but without an operational distribution centre, and not much seems to be happening. Her observation was that most of the refugees have dispersed as well, noting that the international response seems to have died down though there were a few Polish volunteers still around.

I haven't kept up with what's happening in the cities, though I do hear stories that there is a struggle. I decided to write to my point person at Sichów, a resident who speaks English and maintains a chat room for all our other guests. She replied:

> It is very sad. I know many Ukrainians who are returning home because they have run out of money or because they cannot find affordable housing. I heard a story from friends about a woman with a six-year-old child who recently returned to Kharkiv and died the next day. Her husband does not know how to live on. And I understand that the Poles will not always be so kind to us, though for four months they have helped in every possible way.

She is right. Charity runs its course. Even worse, I think about the victims of the concentration camps as they were on no one's radar except for the few and those few could do nothing.

The Poles are already tired. I didn't have the heart to tell her that but I'm beginning to see the subtle signs of vexation. The first sign is the identification of 'the other.' But I am too tired today and my back has gone out (which is no great surprise) so with the energy I do have, I'd like to express what these times and circumstances mean to me in a way that has been influenced by one of my heroines: Alma Rose, the niece of Gustav Mahler.

Alma Rose was the orchestra leader of the 'Girls in the Band' or women's orchestra at Birkenau. Among these courageous and talented women, was the famous cellist Anita Lasker-Wallfisch.

Alma Rose did not survive the war but until the day she succumbed, she resisted through music. They say she was tough on the women and wouldn't put up with laziness or bad performances. I believe she was like this because she was protecting them. One story I remember from my many visits to Birkenau is about a young musician who had to perform as she watched her brother through the window, being marched to the gas chamber. Rose was especially brutal with these tears, as she knew that this dear girl would be right behind him, if she didn't control herself and get her emotions in check. The hierarchy at Bierkenau was not lost on Alma. She knew exactly who to please in order to safeguard her orchestra which is a fascinating story.

None of us here are in harm's way. We are playing outside with the children, enjoying the summer sun, staying up late, watching movies, doing all the things you do at home. The only difference is that you are at home but none of our guests are. Every day, they have to decide how they will survive another day without loved ones, without a home, with a country under attack, living under the weight of their whole lives in question as to the next step.

Every day, without exception, I sit in my chair and I imagine: what if I couldn't go anywhere? What if there was no place to go?

The end of the text from Anastasia (the woman who oversees our chat group) is: "Life stopped on February 24th. And I can't imagine how people live in the Ukraine now. They hear sirens every day, bomb explosions, see the terrible consequences of the use of weapons and must accept that they have nowhere to go."

As difficult a practice as this is, to practice 'what if there were no place to go', because there is naturally no way to answer this question, it does humble me to such a degree that it quickens me; it strengthens my will and my commitment to stay the course alongside each and every one in exile. Dear Alma, one of my angels. You never made it home again to Vienna.

July 12, 2022
Day 139

The weather has turned suddenly to autumn. I'm wearing my sweater and scouring through books of poetry and remembering books I once had, like "Of Woman Born" and "The Yellow Wallpaper" that I gave away in a fit of passion to other women whom I thought needed them, but now wishing I had them in hand to thumb through their pages, far reaching in their wisdom as they are, for I have nothing myself terribly profound to say today.

Room 11: Anastasia, her sister and their mother are returning to the Ukraine on Thursday. Paul and Jordan will drive them to the Polish border town of Przemyśl where they plan to take a train to Lviv, then to Zaporizhia. Their men-folk are waiting there. Plus the cat. Yes, I know. Zaporizhia is under viscous attacks the past few days, but they've been told that it's relatively calm now and they're only returning to pack their things and then move west. It will take a few weeks for the whole process to complete itself before they will be one family again, living in Lviv. This is the story I will carry close to heart until they write from their new home. It's a risk, but perhaps a more calculated one with Russian eyes elsewhere for the moment. The other residents are wary and there are tears of concern.

The roads are unpredictable. There are land mines along many of them. And how far will they have to travel alone or on public transport before their husbands and father reunite with them?

I understand why they are moving back. Ksenia needs to take an entrance exam for the university or else lose a whole year of school, but I'm not sure if this is the motivation of their decision, at least, not in its entirety. They are homesick. They miss their husbands and father. How could they not? Are they even completely conscious of why they left a protected space for one of potential danger; grave danger?

As Paul would say, "This is not the right question to ask." Not the right question because it either has no answer or the answer is unknown to all participating parties.

So what's my question? The truth is, I don't have an answerable question. I only have unanswerable ones. Like this one, for example: Are governments necessary? In true Tolstoyan fashion I beg the question because as far as I can tell, they breed patriarchy, grandiosity and patriotism, all of which cause dreadful wars, brutality, the killing of innocent people, most of whom are women, children and the vulnerable. They make laws to possess and occupy, but not to honour and respect. Is it any wonder why we live in such violent times?

When a young boy sees his mother treated disrespectfully, abused at home by men, and then must witness her acceptance of such treatment, it will ultimately condition him to accept violence. We are devolving at the present time in our attitudes of apathy and inertia and the system in which we live is broken. There is no dependable leadership on the global stage. From where I stand, women all over the world are at risk. They and their children have become the scapegoat for what the collective cannot bear to look at within itself; therefore, it must control with an even tighter grip.

Meanwhile, the new face of those in exile, is of those who are being asked to leave their 'host home' for a variety of reasons. Some hosts claim to be tired and want the exiles out. Five months is long enough, generous enough without much thought given to their vulnerability. We also hear stories of great tension mounting in tight quarters. But whatever the reason, this weekend we are receiving a grandmother and her thirteen-year-old grandson whose mother is still in Bucha. They will take Diana's room, where our new born stayed.

Following, we expect another family escaping from the Donbas region, senior parents with their daughter. They will stay in Room 11 where Anastasia had been. So this is us again, at full capacity.

I don't know what sent me to bookshelves looking for Rich and Gilman, I suppose the whole idea of 'motherhood to mothering' did. Does anyone read these books anymore? Do young mothers talk about boredom and the feeling of confinement?

I remember when Zach was small and I really did enjoy being around him. He had this infectious laugh and was quite entertaining. But then there were times when I didn't enjoy it and I didn't want to play but wanted to read and write and travel and be alone without the responsibility for another, yet there we were, the two of us, both in these dual embryonic states, each growing into our own evolving consciousness. How does one stay the course these days?

It's inherent in my nature to mother and to care for another, so I woke up every day committed to this little stick of a boy who hadn't a care in the world, frequently having to remind myself that I was a good enough mother when I wasn't so engaged or cheerful.

The test came again, in his adult years when he needed me once more, when the stakes were high as to whether we would succeed or not, but, by grace, Paul and the amazing family we have, there was a victory.

In a world where the inhabitants are increasingly isolated and psychotic, one has to wonder if the absence of care and commitment to care is one of the missing pieces to this puzzle. When an over culture hasn't systems in place for care or to care, then the whole of society reflects this – in some instances even justifies the premature turning out onto the street those in need of long term assistance.

It's a big question, the question of how we mother ourselves, how we mother each other. The question of sacrifice is invariably the first obstacle one encounters or the self-serving viewpoint of 'what's in it for me' 'can't be bothered' and this I fear is leading us down a dead-end road.

All this to say, that it's not always easy, but when did easy become the goal?

As Jung pointed out, one holds the opposites until there is a transcendence. What does that look like in an ordinary, domestic setting if we were to stay the course of motherhood to mothering?

It looks like a vibrant and healthy home, in which family members are at liberty to express themselves, their shadow, their fears and their aspirations. It's a place for good moods and bad ones. A place of misunderstandings and reconciliations. It's a container for success and failure alike. It's a place of love and acceptance.

July 27, 2022
Day 154

> Art where really understood, is the province of every human being. It is simply a question of doing things, anything, well. It is not an outside, extra thing. Where the artist is alive in any person, whatever his kind of work may be, he becomes an inventive, searching, daring, self-expressing creature. He becomes interesting to other people. He disturbs, upsets, enlightens and he opens ways for a better understanding. Where those who are not artists are trying to close the book, he opens it, shows there are still more pages possible... He does not have to be a painter or sculptor to be an artist. He can find work in any medium. He simply has to find the gain in the work itself, not outside it. Museums of art will not make a country an art country. But where there is the art spirit there will be precious works to fill museums. Better still, there will be the happiness that is in the making. Art tends towards balance, order, judgement of relative values, the laws of growth, the economy of living...Very good things for anyone to be interested in. Robert Henri, American Painter and Teacher (1865-1929).

I was talking with an old friend yesterday via Skype and as we were hanging up, she commented to some now forgotten question: "I wouldn't know. You don't keep in touch anymore."

It was a very painful reminder that my life has changed in ways that will never again return to its previous landscape. There is a profound loss in sacrifice, where giving of yourself is only the first step.

Before the war started, Paul and I were invited by our nephew to Kurozweki for a special Valentine's Day Dinner. It was a very exciting evening for us because Andrew offered to ferry us both ways so that we could drink champagne without having to appoint a designated driver. The place was packed with young and old romantic hopefuls; all their dreams crowded into one night of celebration. That night, Andrew asked if we were seriously going to open our doors to refugees should there be war. Paul, being droll, said that if a bus full of Ukrainians were to pull up to the house, he would certainly invite them inside. We never expected the presage of such a comment to literally manifest at our doorstep less than two weeks later. One opens the door.

Five months into sheltering, I can honestly say nothing compares to the grinding down one bears in the new responsibility of human care. If we accept this responsibility because it knocked at the door, it will change everything about our lives in much the same way one is changed when a child is born. The sacrifice to the child is great and can't help but alter our external circumstances as a result.

Last night, Jordan made us a delicious dinner of slow roasted cherry tomatoes, toasted ciabatta, a fried egg, basil and a touch of Roquefort. The community sits at the same table throughout the day, but sharing only the lunchtime meal; breakfast and dinner are what individual families make for themselves. Several others joined us in conversation, which at first was breezy and quite cheerful. We were discussing the upcoming plans for the circus in mid-August. I am writing a play which will be translated into Ukrainian. Others will be making costumes. Friends coming from America will bring face paint, instruments and masks.

It was an untroubled gathering until, in a word, a glance, a pause, as one can never pinpoint the exact moment it all changes. "Books are to be burned in the oblast (regions) around Kharkiv." Apparently, in regions under Russian occupation, all Ukrainian text books written after 1992 are mandated to be burned. These books are no longer valid for the new curriculum. The Ukrainian language is no longer allowed in schools. Teachers who have been teaching for several decades must now submit to those demands or be charged with collaboration with the enemy. There were a series of other stories mentioned about mothers whose sons are now in Russian prisons. We also heard of how their friends, waiting at a bus stop, were injured by a missile strike. They were taken to a hospital.

What makes it so hard as an observer? One wakes in the morning to people who need something. There is always a need, usually multiple ones. Paul gets by well because he speaks serviceable Russian. I speak kitchen Polish at best. When he is around, things go more smoothly since most guests communicate in Russian but there are those who will only speak Ukrainian which is difficult for either of us to understand. Thus, the day begins. No one has a car, so Paul and I have to run most errands personally. A frequent need is to see a doctor or have a prescription filled. That requires an early morning drive of several miles to the clinic, to stand in line for an appointment. If you're lucky you get an appointment that day, otherwise you return the next day. No longer can you make an appointment by phone. All prescription refills have to be personally signed off by a doctor.

Lately, he's had to drive to Kielce, an hour away to take one to the dentist, another to the hospital for a post op visit, still more to specialists in a particular field of disability, such as epilepsy.

By mid-day, we are usually home from our errands, picking up meds, bread, extra things from shelving to toothpaste. Sometimes, the day is generous and allows us a senior nap, before more errands. Three days a week there is a wholesale food order that must be completed, and a vegetable and fruit order.

There are days when you are so tired you can hardly imagine doing one more thing. And for me, it's done with a translator at hand. Nothing is simple. Conversation is hard. Communication takes the greatest patience, movement through the house is never a solitary stride unless before dawn which hardly ever occurs that I rise so early to make coffee.

Readers want to know the personal stories of our families and I can only deliver to you incomplete ones. To begin, their personal lives are not my business, unless a story is shared and, as you can see, there is literally *always* something lost in translation.

Have I hurt someone's feelings? Sometimes I sit at the table across from another, perhaps it is just the two of us at that moment, and she is crying alone. Do I force an encounter? I can't reach across the table without great awkwardness, so I stay still, looking elsewhere. What good will it do anyway if I know someone so intimately? Is that really the objective of care? Must I know each little detail like some small town gossip and for what? So I can disclose this suffering in a diary?

The high points are easily identifiable. Loss. Loss of home, dignity, rights, language, history, culture, lifestyle, friends, family and pets. That should keep us busy. Contemplating just one, for example, loss of a pet. We've all been there so we know what that feels like.

The stakes are higher in war of course and most of us do not know the effects of this. Loss of home. Loss of place. How to begin again?

There are 35 to 40 residents on any given day depending on capacity. Each one must come to terms in their own way, in their own time as to how to begin again. Even the children.

My task is a different one. A collective one. If you take Jung at his word in *Answer to Job*, then "[Man] He can no longer wriggle out of it [responsibility] on the plea of his littleness and nothingness, for the dark God has slipped the atom bomb and chemical weapons (and I add to this list, bio-warfare) into his hands and given him the power to empty out the apocalyptic vials of wrath on his fellow creatures. Since he has been granted an almost godlike power, he can no longer remain blind and unconscious. He must know something of God's nature and of metaphysical processes if he is to understand himself and thereby achieve gnosis of the Divine."

Ukrainian families are rendered homeless at alarming rates around the globe. Their hosts are tired.

This is not the response nor the action from those who have been cast as observers; our role is to remain strong and to witness. To assist in the care of another human being without needing to know all details. That one suffers is enough. How do I restore myself? I write these diaries, for one, as it is my way of witnessing. I am writing a new fairy tale. I am writing for the children and their circus. I listen to early Baroque music as often as is possible and twice a week to my husband teaching recorder to Olesya. I try to surround myself with beauty. I am moving through the house alongside others, not asking for privacy but asking how I can be of service.

"The only thing that really matters now is whether man can climb up to a higher moral level, to a higher plane of consciousness..." Jung, *Answer to Job.*

I cannot turn my back on this. We must accept this sacrifice as a vehicle to both personal growth and the collective growth of consciousness. So, yes, I have changed and I will never again be the same. But if it means strengthening my commitment to God, if it means understanding better both His nature and my own, if it means, as Jung points out, rising to a higher moral level, then the sacrifice is worth the loss of the old life.

Five new residents arrived last week. Luba and her son, Stefan. And most recently, on Friday, Marina and her eldest son, K. and the youngest, M. who is severely handicapped. He was born four months premature but received poor hospital care. He is now eleven and cannot walk or speak, feed or dress himself. But he does like being wheeled around outside. He's got the sweetest face.

August 7, 2022
Day 165

> Look up to the sky. Ask yourselves: is it yes or
> no? Has the sheep eaten the flower? And you will
> see how everything changes ... And no grown-up
> will ever understand that this is a matter of so
> much importance. *The Little Prince* by Antoine de
> Saint-Exupery.

My nephew is going back to Houston tomorrow because
his best friend is riddled with cancer. Dear Patrick, is
also his priest and mentor, a Taoist priest.

Jordan has been with us since March. His absence
will be acutely noticed. Our time together has been
refreshing, joyful, complicated, difficult at times in
knowing how to pilot circumstances, but overall rich
and memorable. When an adult child returns and blesses
you with this gift of their presence, nothing can compare
to its wealth because all the years of birthday parties,
baseball games, summer holidays, bedtime stories and
the suspense of adolescence are within reach, and yet
all the potential and possibility of their autonomy are
manifesting right before your eyes. It's as if you get to
see the bud bloom twice and before you know it, they
are teaching you about life. I will miss him.

It has been an unforgettable week. It has been life-
ing, as Jordan would say. When pain and suffering and
joy and fear blend with peals of uncontrollable laughter
and anger and confusion, discomfort and hope all in
motion at the same time: that's what life does, that's
what life is. Life is life-ing itself.

The highlight of the week has been our American
visitors. Melanie and Betsy arrived at Sichów on

Tuesday bearing five full suitcases of art supplies, toiletries, material for our seamstresses, and clothes. The two girl powerhouses reminded me of my home and America and the side of our culture that I most admire and appreciate. The irrepressible positive nature in each, their 'can-do' attitude, their willingness to roll up their sleeves and work alongside any task regardless of its demand, was refreshing to say the least. More than this, it was a boost of energy we didn't even know we needed until we got it. For weeks ahead of their visit, they organised groups of other friends who worked with them in assembling the individual kits of art supplies for the children and the toiletry bags that looked like they came from Bergdorf Goodman. The material and textiles lovingly hand-picked, the cash donations, the time spent by each person who contributed illustrates the generosity of the American spirit.

Stefan and Ania hosted our American guests so thoughtfully with delicious dinners, fantastic wines and conversations against a backdrop of gardens and vineyards. They will take back some lovely memories of their trip to Poland.

(But I can't end it here, no 'Not yet, not yet! the White Rabbit hastily interrupted, "There's a great deal to come before that!" There are cookies and pizza to talk about.)

We co-host a Mud Day event every summer and one of the food booths is a cafe selling homemade cookies, cake and coffee.

Melanie and Betsy, in unison said: 'Oh. We'll make cookies ahead of time and put them in the freezer. Then all you have to do is pull them out and bake them that morning.'

I was thrilled. Two American women coming to Poland to make chocolate chip cookies for a Mud Day event; it doesn't get any better than that, so off to the store I went before anyone had time to reconsider.

I returned around 11:00, when the kitchen was in full frenzy. Food supplies were being delivered and unloaded, cooks were preparing for the afternoon meal, while the children hovered around the bowl set aside for the cookies, attentively guarding their square footage so as not to be overlooked when it came time to have a turn at the electric mixer, the four or five dogs indiscriminately circling the ankles of those who might accidentally drop a spare sausage, and it was in this atmosphere that I left the bags on the counter for Melanie and Betsy to get started.

It was a second-class miracle, I thought, when not only did the marinade get made for the sliced chicken burgers, but the homemade mayonnaise and the cookies all at the same time with dogs and children alike under foot.

Betsy invited me to taste the cookie dough before the chocolate went in, to which I eagerly accepted. I lifted the spoon to my mouth and said, 'Hmmm ... I like them, they're not too sweet.' 'No,' she agreed, both of us looking somewhat puzzled but it tasted like chocolate chip cookie dough I thought to myself.

It wasn't long before we realized that perhaps we should make another batch to make it even easier for our Mud Day event.

As Betsy was starting on the second one, she picked up a bag of 'Bulka Tarta' and asked, 'What is this?' That's bread crumbs. It suddenly dawned on both of us that she had used bread crumbs instead of brown sugar for the cookie dough. I couldn't stop laughing. I was laughing uncontrollably. It was one of those moments when literally all is lost in translation, including your cookie dough.

This did not stop us from baking a few. We unanimously agreed that we had to taste this variation on one of America's national treasures. Perhaps we were onto something.

As it turned out, we were pleasantly surprised. The bread crumbs were not seasoned and so finely ground that it was like adding additional flour and the chocolate is strong that it made up for the absence of the sugar. But you do have to cook it a bit longer and it needs to cool completely before consuming.

No one will be the wiser. They were yummy, if for no other reason than energetically they were full of so much love and laughter.

After an afternoon rest, here they come again to make individual pizzas with the children. And not just any pizza, but boutique pizzas. Each child had their square of parchment paper laid in front of them alongside all the bowls of toppings from which to choose. Tomato sauce, basil, mozzarella, sliced salami, onions and peppers.

Thank you Melanie. Thank you Betsy. It's been a long time since I have felt as sentimental about America as I did during the few days you were here.

You were a hit with everyone, especially the seamstresses who made you each a Doll Motanka. The doll is an amulet that protects the family. It represents female power. Inner power.

The climate of the house was pensive and quiet after you left. I wouldn't know for certain if this is what people were feeling, but it seemed to me like everyone here knew you were going home again; a place where, for the time being, isn't safe for them to go.

To believe in fairy tales and monsters and angels and teddy bears that talk seems to me a good way to be in the world. Nobody has to know. Why must adults be so dull? They start wars with all of their knowledge and boredom.

It seems to me that everything is a waste of time', he remarked one day as he walked dejectedly home from school. 'I can't see the point in learning to solve useless problems, or subtracting turnips from turnips, or knowing where Ethiopia is or how to spell February.' And since no one bothered to explain otherwise, he regarded the process of seeking knowledge as the greatest waste of all time. *The Phantom Toll Booth*, Norman Juster.

August 15, 2022
Day 173

Suffering, of course, can lead us in either of two directions: (1) it can make us very bitter and cause us to shut down, or (2) it can make us wise, compassionate, and utterly open, because our hearts have been softened, or perhaps because we feel as though we have nothing more to lose. Suffering often takes us to the very edge of our inner resources where we "fall into the hands of the living God" (Hebrews 10:31), even when we aren't sure we believe in God! We must all pray for the grace of this second path of softening and opening. My opinion is that this is the very meaning of the phrase "deliver us from evil" in the Our Father (Lord's Prayer). In this statement, we aren't asking to avoid suffering. It is as if we are praying, "When big trials come, God, hold on to me, and don't let me turn bitter or blaming"–which is an evil that leads to so many other evils.

"Struggling with one's own shadow self, facing interior conflicts and moral failures, undergoing rejection and abandonment, daily humiliations, or any form of limitation: all are gateways into deeper consciousness and the flowering of the soul.
Richard Rohr's Daily Meditation, from the Center for Action and Contemplation

The daily meditation pages of Richard Rohr this week took on the theme of the two universal paths of suffering and love, which he points out are part of most human lives. St. Therese of Lisieux reminds us that ... 'suffering alone gives birth to souls.'

Today is the feast of the Assumption of Mary, an observed holiday in Poland. It celebrates Our Lady's union with the Trinity.

In *Mysterium Coniunctionis* Carl Jung writes in a footnote:

> A Catholic writer says of the Assumption: 'Nor, would it seem, is the underlying motif itself even peculiarly Christian; rather it would seem to be but one expression of a universal archetypal pattern, which somehow responds to some deep and widespread human need, and which finds other similar expressions in countless myths and rituals, poems and pictures, practices and even philosophies, all over the globe. *Victor White, The Scandal of the Assumption.*

How accessible is Mary? I have a long history with her which I shared with my analyst and my most intimate relationships. Let me be very clear that I am quite aware of her archetypal status, but know from my personal relationship with her that she is so much more.

If you would, dear reader, consider with me for the moment that before Mary became an archetype or God-bearer she was a Jewish mother. Have you ever known a Jewish mother? I can tell you I have had the good fortune to have known many and some very well. They are a force, especially where their children are concerned. There are many worn-out, hackneyed stereotypes of the Jewish mother which I ask you to disregard as they are pointless to the subject. We are moving too fast in this world to adequately assimilate what is happening to us psychologically and when that happens, we must go back. What did you miss when you were thirteen? What was happening in your life, what signs were there that you might be able to see now, more clearly from a distance? This is the kind of psychological work I'm talking about. Why is it important? Because the world is on fire and the target is humanity.

I want to go back to Mary as a Jewish mother and talk to her about real life and suffering and love and obligation and faith and her traditions as a religious woman. I want to know how she managed the humiliation of being pregnant out of wedlock. How did she keep strong when the village shunned her? I want to know how she felt having no home in which to give birth to her first born child. She hadn't midwives nor mother, nor sisters nor neighbours to assist her, but had to endure the impoverished conditions of where animals slept and remain faithful that she was worthy of God's love in spite of her circumstances. I want to know the suffering of her flight into Egypt. I want to know how she survived in a foreign land caring for her children, not knowing the language of her hosts or having any familiarity with their customs. I want to know about her return and the joy she must have anticipated upon hearing that Herod was dead and her family was no longer in danger.

Before Mary became an archetype, she was a Jewish Mother.

Catholics believe that Mary was free from original sin from the moment of her conception, thus the Immaculate Conception and thus upon the completion of an earthly life, she enters heavenly glory by grace. Did she know this? Did everyone who knew her know this too? Did Mary Magdalene with whom she clung so close at the cross, know this? Did the other Mary's who gathered there know?

In these times of the oppression, abuse, exploitation and slaughter of women, I believe it is a mistake to exclusively spiritualise the archetypes with whom we so desperately need human contact. It is a slow and carefully trodden path into which one ventures, seeking the humanity within the archetype, for she is the God-bearer and has the power of the Divine, but she is also a mother who understands human suffering.

Our last Mud Day event of the season was on Saturday. The families who joined us had a fantastic time, outside, rolling around in the mud, splashing around in water, running, jumping, climbing, playing ... a child's pastime, a child's human right.

Ania offered cookies and sweet things with coffee from the cafe. The house opened up for lunch and dinner putting forth a feast of vegetarian and vegan options.

The closing event was a theatrical one. Stefan read from his own mother's children's book, *Leśne Wędrówki*. about the forest and its animals. The Ukrainian residents animated the story with music, singing and dancing, bringing it to life to the delight and squeals of both child and adult alike. It was especially memorable because Stefan's children and grandchildren were there to honour her. Maria Radziwiłł – Wąsowicz endured five long years of war without her own mother, Zofia, who was in Ravensbruck and her father in Majdanek.

For those few, blessed moments, we could forget there was a war raging in a country only hours from here. For those few blessed moments everyone could lapse into a temporary state of magical thinking that they could go home after the party was over.

I try not to engage in conversation about the war because invariably there comes a point in which pragmatism and rationalization overtake compassionate thinking and nothing assaults my senses worse than this. To think that we can manoeuvre our way around this situation without first and foremost recognizing that we don't even have an inkling about the impact upon those lives whose homes have been destroyed, whose family members have been lost forever, whose livelihoods usurped; and it doesn't bring any satisfaction, not one iota, to say that WWII was worse. Not one. Because whether you are surgically removed or removed with the blunt edge of an axe, the end result is the same.

Ultimately, the family is no longer the functioning unit it was before the terror struck. There is no container left for its traditions, its language, its culture and its stories. Everyone is on the run, mothers still cling tight to their little ones. And even though the members of my family by marriage survived the war and went on to live conventional lives, they were never the same.

Ilse Weber was Tommy's mother. They were for a while at Terezin before they were both moved to Auschwitz. They were murdered in the gas chamber. Ilse also wrote children's books and books of poetry. She was such a talented woman and we lost her and her dear boy and for what? What have we gained as a 'civilisation', from the slaughter of Ilse and Tommy? And the loss of all the mothers and children, all over the globe. How are we a better humanity because of this loss? I am curious.

Gala is one of the residents here. She is a child psychologist by profession and an artist. She organises artistic and outdoor activities for the children whose mothers must be very grateful to her to have a bit of a break during the day.

On Friday night, a few weeks ago, she told me that the windows of her family home had been blown out.

She said that she remembers leaving an open book on the table. Now with all the dirt and water from the rain that has accumulated inside the house, she imagines that out of the spine of the book grows a long, thick root, that stretches into the outside by way of the open window, giving rise to beautiful flowers.

August 20, 2022
Day 178

HOPE

> "Pani Amber, we must be optimistic."
> Andrei Pechenizkyi, Masha's Grandfather

Every day at Sichów is a potential diary entry but this one came out of the blue, sent on the wings of an angel.

Masha, one of our resident teenagers who is also a budding film maker, sent me a link to her new video, filmed here, outside under the trees. It's called "Going Home".

The lyrics read:

> When I will come home
> War won't end in you
> We will create something new
> Famous and great
> So that it does not come to the city again
>
> You and me will be us again
> Flowers that have not been plucked
> Suns that in winter weren't afraid
> People in the city who loved
>
> You and me will be us again
> Flowers that have not been plucked
> Suns that in winter weren't afraid
> People in the city which loved
>
> When you will come home
> I will put in new glass lanterns

You will smile at them, native and so alien
You'll say that it's most difficult to be
To be people at war

You and me will be us again
Flowers that have not been plucked
Suns that in winter weren't afraid
People in the city who loved

You and me will be us again
Flowers that have not been plucked
Suns that in winter weren't afraid
People in the city which loved

All of us are here together in hope while we, work, create, give of ourselves, despair, irritable at times and question the future. What touches me so about Masha's "Going Home" is that in spite of all of her dreams dashed at sixteen, she still goes outside to make a short film. Of course Masha's dreams are not lost forever, we all know that, even so, they have been dramatically rearranged and while she could choose to spend her time depressed and inactive, she decides rather to make a short film about homesickness. She wakes up with hope and she creates.

In her film – *No Toys*, we catch a glimpse of her world in the Ukraine before the war destroyed it.

Fr. Thomas Keating writes, "... to have no hope is to be inhuman. To be able to survive with any degree of endurance requires some ray of hope."

In Elie Wiesel's Nobel Prize winning speech on December 11, 1986, he tells a Hasidic legend. It's certainly worth looking up to re-read. But for purposes of this entry, I have chosen the following:

... the importance of friendship is in man's ability to transcend his condition. I love it most of all because it emphasizes the mystical power of memory. Without memory, our existence would be barren and opaque, like a prison cell into which no light penetrates; like a tomb which rejects the living. Memory saved the Besht*, and if anything can, it is memory that will save humanity. For me, hope without memory is like memory without hope. Just as man cannot live without dreams, he cannot live without hope. If dreams reflect the past, hope summons the future. Does this mean that our future can be built on a rejection of the past? Surely such a choice is not necessary. The two are not incompatible. The opposite of the past is not the future but the absence of future; the opposite of the future is not the past but the absence of past. The loss of one is equivalent to the sacrifice of the other. A recollection. The time: After the war. The place: Paris. A young man struggles to readjust to life. His mother, his father, his small sister are gone. He is alone, on the verge of despair, and yet he does not give up. On the contrary, he strives to find a place among the living. He acquires a new language. He makes a few friends who, like himself, believe that the memory of evil will serve as a shield against evil; that the memory of death will serve as a shield against death. This he must believe in order to go on.

---

* Besht concerns a legendary Jewish tradition passed down orally.

On Wednesday, we will receive another five people, two mothers and their children and while we only have one room left, which is not big enough for all of them, the residents in the room next door offered to share their space. They are coming from Zaporizhia where the war is getting worse. The shelling in Kharkiv is also relentless from what our guests say. Unfortunately, it's less reported by the mainstream media where a war weariness has set in.

August 28, 2022
Day 186

The Stakes are High. Day after Day

Andrei Pechenizkyi is a resident. He is here with his
wife, two daughters and two granddaughters. He is a
painter, an illustrator and writer. In his 1982 short story,
*The Underground,** he writes:

> Life in the underground followed its own laws,
> there was its own regularity, preordained by the
> electronic master, which did not entice anybody,
> but also did not surprise...and these laws, this
> minute-by-minute journey, which had taken in
> millions of human destinies without a murmur,
> were no longer the privilege of the chosen few;
> the underground, eliminating the right of choice
> ... we're starting to slip out of our seats one by
> one and life on the tube goes on, our lives go
> on, as long as you're allowed, and you live to see
> the day in a fog, ... that prickly subterranean
> wind is literally churning through you, blowing
> you up into a cry of terror, even though you do
> not understand where it comes from and what
> you have grown into such an all-consuming
> fear, and in those moments the main thing is
> to escape from the black subterranean torrent
> you squirm in your seat, but there is no escape
> from the poisonous wind ...

---

* *Compendium of Science Fiction*, Issue 26th (Moscow:
Znanie, 1982. Andrei Pechenizkyi, Metro

Ukraine was part of the Soviet Union when the protagonist in *The Underground* was confined to the order of the train and the schedule it imposed, a TV in every car, and the factories to where he and the other passengers were dispatched, back and forth, day in and day out. "... because day after day we meet in these carriages, and these carriages divide our lives into three almost equal parts: work, sleep, a trip, three and a half hours in one direction, the same for the return trip, with a few minutes to stretch your legs, walk down the passage to the lift, have dinner with your wife and say goodnight, nothing else to talk to her about, and it is all repeated day after day."

Maybe the strategies of an autocracy have changed, certainly they've been modernized, but the purpose remains the same – a government in which one person has the power to impose unlimited authority over others.

The Underground evokes a distinct Kafkaesque atmosphere as the protagonist draws the reader deeper into his internal dialogue.

The law is the law, and the law forbids employers to contract people from their own area, only equidistant, not less than three hours by electric train, and there is nothing we can do about it, because it is the law, and breaking it brings too severe a punishment for any of us to dare to do it, and we do not need it, and it's of no use either because none of us would know what to do with ourselves if the situation changed, and our workplace was also chosen by computers, and we believe in the wisdom of their decisions, because we have nothing else to believe in, nothing else is available to us.

In her appearance at the Nanovic Forum, 2022, Anne Applebaum** makes the statement: "Putin has also been very clear that for him, this is also an existential war. He sees the existence of a sovereign, independent, democratic Ukraine, a Ukraine that has integrated with Europe and the world, as a personal threat to him and to his power."

She also said: "Everything that happens tomorrow, depends on the decisions we make today." Such a simple thing to say and yet it carries with it the greatest wisdom.

So here we are on this day, today. 'Oh, bother,' as Winnie the Pooh would say. What decisions will we make? How crucial they are to our tomorrow.

Wednesday was Ukrainian Independence Day which we celebrated with robust enthusiasm. We feasted on pizza and burgers, red wine and beer. And this day gave rise to the next day Thursday, Wednesday's tomorrow, and on that day we presented our play, "Happy Town". I was the witch and Paul was the Dragon. Masha was the narrator. All the children had a part. Yulia was the director and Gala the set designer. A resounding round of applause for the seamstresses, Oksana, Nadia, and to Marla Hughes and Carly Hodes who came all the way from Los Angeles.

** *The Twilight of Democracy: The Seductive Lure of Authoritarianism* (Doubleday, 2020).

At the beginning of last week, there was notable confusion about how the play would find its feet. I was very concerned, of course, because we only had 48 hours within which to pull off a production that included masks, costumes, set design, music and dance and we were still in the rehearsal room.

But with eight bags of old sheets, curtains, tablecloths and pillows, Gala Pechenizka, Andrei's daughter, and her sister Yulia made what I can only call magic. For $135, there emerged a backdrop and elaborate costumes.

Did we even dream that the children were to write their own story and perform it?

A place called Happy Town is under threat from a dragon that has grown three heads. The residents of Happy Town, a pig, horse, bear and hedgehog call on a witch to save them from the dragon. No, the children didn't know how this was to be done. They called on a witch who invoked the elements of air, fire, earth, water and tree.

"What's to be done with the dragon in the end?" I wondered.

"Kill it," the children emphatically said.

But in the end they didn't.

Instead they popped its extra heads with the result that the dragon changed and became a positive force.

A happy ending. Wishful thinking? It's a message of hope that the balance will one day be restored, so that they can return to Happy Town.

Every day, there is something that must be put back together. Hurt feelings, missed cues, misunderstandings. We don't have any place else to go but here for the moment so we must hold tight to the day, focus on what we are doing, and then allow for tomorrow to do its job.

The stakes are high because we don't have an inroad into a political solution. It's not something we can influence. However, what we can do is write, paint, cook, sew, clean, put on plays, go to the lake and try as best as is possible to make decisions today that will make tomorrow happen in a way that benefits us all.

September 2, 2022
Day 191

A Letter to My Mother-in-Law, Rose Popiel Kieniewicz*

Dear Rose,

I asked all the wrong questions about Ruszcza**. I asked you stupid questions, like, were you afraid, what did you do during the day, were you bored, how did you manage to secretly move your furnishings into Krakow and beyond, to Warsaw, did you often hear artillery fire? What ridiculous questions these were. Why did you not reproach me and say, "Listen, don't ask me these impertinent questions. If you want to know what it's like to live five years during a war in a house with 40 displaced people driven from their homes by force, ask me smart questions like how did we manage to maintain a sense of emotional equilibrium? Or how

---

* Rose Popiel was born in Wójcza, a small village about 20 kilometres from Sichów. Rose's mother and her mother's sister married first cousins. Rose's first cousin, Zofia married Krzysztof Radziwiłł and they settled here at Sichów.

** In 1939, a young newlywed, Rose Popiel Kieniewicz, said goodbye to her husband, Polish Officer Henryk Kieniewicz, on the platform of the Kraków Główny train station. She didn't see him again until Christmas Eve, 1945 . During the war years their manor home, received as Rose's dowry, was transformed into a shelter for refugees. She was only nineteen.

After the war, she and Henry moved to Scotland where they settled until the end of their days. Henry came back to Poland only after the fall of the Soviet Union. They had three children, Theresa (Terenia), Paul, and Mary.

did we renew our faith, day in and day out? How did we remain optimistic? Ask me smart questions." I wish that I could go back to those days when we poured over the old photographs and have another chance to ask them.

I miss you. Everywhere I turn these days, you're there. Just as it was for me on my first trip to Poland when I cried everywhere I went. Do you remember me telling you about that? You thought it was very funny, though a little bit silly that I would fall apart like that. Your whole family must have thought Paul's wife was disturbed, that she kept bursting into floods of tears and then ran for the nearest bathroom. It was especially difficult for me at Gontyna. Ciocia Zosia thought I was unhinged. At one point, she said in a way unique only Ciocia Zosia, "What's wrong with her!" There was so much of you still in that house, in the furnishings, outside where you gardened, and the sun room where your father died.

These sudden hysterics must have been troubling to the observer, but all the stories of the war came hastening back; there was no place in Krakow, no place in Warsaw where I visited that I didn't see a piece of you or a piece of Ruszcza. The image of you at twenty-four, loading up a bryczka*** and sneaking into Krakow, at great risk to your life to distribute your belongings among family members, is to this day quite a powerful one. (I want you to know that I still have the picture of Wójcza. It hangs on the wall in the library, right next to the Mehoffer study of Our Lady. Don't worry. They are safe with me.)

I wasn't prepared for this war, even though for Paul and I it's of no direct consequence. Not like it was for

---

*** A dogcart

you in 1939 when the violence and the threat of death was around every corner. One never knew from hour to hour what might be encountered. This is a different kind of war today for those of us living in Poland. Russia has invaded Ukraine, not us, and is determined to reclaim this country. Putin, not unlike Stalin in your day, imposes his own maniacal and deranged will upon anyone who stands in the way of achieving his goal.

There's so much I want to tell you. We are living at Sichów, sheltering 40 refugees from Ukraine. You must be surprised to hear this news after so many years of peace and even more surprised that we ended up at Sichów.

Our cousin, Stefan, Zofia Radziwiłł's grandson, found a book with your name and the signatures of you and your sisters in it. You had come for a birthday party but Jaś stayed home, probably because of his studies and Józio was just a baby, so it was only the girls who signed the book.

Generous donations have kept the wolf from the door but winter is coming and Russia is up to no good: they have turned off the gas to Germany and who knows what that will mean for Poland and the rest of Europe for that matter.

I never asked you how you kept warm at Ruszcza. You were only nineteen and a newlywed when you opened your doors to those in need. Your husband had been captured and you didn't know at first his whereabouts nor anything about his safety. Had he been injured? Had he been killed? My God, I never thought to ask these questions. Nor did I ask who was in the house helping you for those first few months of pandemonium.

From the few diary entries Terenia**** found, you did have food stores in the cellar which must have kept you going at least through the first winter, replenished in subsequent years from the fields, I can only presume. I know you were hungry, and I know you were trying to hold on to what you had, from what you write in your diary about filling up the sugar bowl only half way.

Blessedly, we have plenty of food and we're warm for the moment. Everyone here is active, cooking, cleaning; the children are in school and the teenagers are enrolled in online studies.

So what makes my heart long so to be with you again, to consult with you and have you by my side to reassure me? I lose my way. I get scared and I hate other people sometimes. All the things that would disappoint you in a person. I confess I'm at fault.

I am writing to ask for your prayers. Terenia is praying for us and there are many scattered around the globe who are also praying. I understand we are named on several prayer lists. What a blessing, my life.

As I was saying, it's a different kind of war on the outside, but on the inside, it is the same one. It could easily be 1939 again. Everyone here has lost their country for the moment as did you and Henry, forced to leave Poland. Everyone here has lost their living space. They've had to leave behind their belongings, their pets, their way of life, their routine, their jobs, all that was familiar in the world to them. They have left behind brothers, fathers, husbands, neighbours, and those too sick to make the journey.

At first, there was an outpouring of compassion, later turned to bitter resentment among many. Just as

****Terenia is Paul's elder sister.

it was for you and Henry settling in Scotland that first year, there were those who did not want you there and some who made it difficult for you to adjust. There was that awful woman in Bankfoot who insisted you keep a newborn quiet. Honestly.

Of course not everyone behaves this way but there are those among some locals for whom the Ukrainians are a visible irritation. And in all fairness, to have a million people load up an infrastructure not capable of handling them would realistically cause frustration.

I admit to the complexities of such a situation but I also feel the way it's handled is not in good form either and that's what brings out the worst in me. Paul's sister calls it 'compassion fatigue.' Really? How can one tire of compassion? Is this not what keeps us connected to God?

There must have been things that drove you crazy during the war that sent you to seek the help of Heaven to overcome. Why didn't I ask that question? There must have been conflicts in the house. How did a nineteen-year-old manage to quell these tensions? And I have no idea what external obstacles you faced. I know the church next door offered a great comfort to you but then I don't know what the neighbours were like, whether they caused you any sleepless nights. I know German army officers parked themselves in the house. That couldn't have been easy for you.

I lose my temper frequently because I'm always remembering you, dear girl, heading for Scotland, pregnant and looking for shelter and a way to make a living in a language you know not a word. Fortunately you had Henry, as he survived. But these women do not have their husbands. They are alone with their children. Yes, I thought that would break your heart.

We are quick today to judge another and quick to insist that people move on and start a new life and forget about their country or go the hell back. We have forgotten and we don't want to be inconvenienced. Very few pause in meditation and think what it would feel like to be standing in the kitchen, drinking the first cup of coffee of the day, on a Thursday morning in late February and hear the missiles rain down. The disorientation. The panic. The random grab for whatever is within in reach. What about the dogs? What about the baby's favourite toy? Can't find it? Leave it. A doctor's appointment this afternoon. Forget about it. Forget about everything except running for the border, by foot, by bus, by train, by car.

We've had dancers, professional artists, school administrators, psychologists and teachers arrive at the doorstep. We have teenagers, their dreams aborted. Some of the more recent arrivals are clearly depressed and this worries me terribly.

The philosophy here at The Cross Border House*****
is to create together an environment for those living in exile, the opportunity to stabilize their systems so that they can once more think about their future. They can begin to plan. It's impossible to plan in an atmosphere of panic. Landlords in the cities are wary of leasing to Ukrainians as they regard them as high-risk tenants. Jobs are in short supply unless you're willing to grab a toilet brush and get to it and there's nothing wrong with that but the income yielded by such a job is not going to add up fast enough to put down the money for an apartment that a landlord is not likely to lease to

*****The Cross Border House is the name we have chosen for our community efforts here at Sichów.

you anyway. What does one do in the meantime. The Ukrainians without a place to live are begging space from other Ukrainian families who did manage to acquire lodging. Then there is the question of schools for the children and, oh yes, the language. Not unlike it was for you and Henry. Alone, without anything familiar around you. What was it you used to say: "If anyone had told me that by the time I was 25 I'd be living in Scotland, I'd say they were from the moon."

The model here is to provide shelter, food, clothing, and other basic needs such as toiletries and medicine. But it's so much more than that. It's a place of psychological well-being where one can pick up where they left off in Ukraine. Naturally, not in the exact way but in a way that nourishes ones soul. For anyone who was an artist, wishes to paint or to draw, the gallery welcomes them. If one were a seamstress, then the sewing room invites one to take material and thread and machine and create something useful. And these spaces develop organically along with the community. At first we thought the gallery would only be for the professional painters, but in fact it has become so much more to the other residents: children's activities and drawing classes, a space for our plays and concerts, a quiet workspace for others.

We are criticised for this model, as the hard-core facts of life are bearing down from a society that could give a fig about the soul and thinks us privileged for even considering such a way of being in the world. Why should we be able to live like this when other people are not? That's another irrelevant question.

Most people don't have the luxury of designing their own lives. They have to work at jobs they don't like, live in spaces that cost them most of their income with little left over for recreational activities, in relationships they perhaps only tolerate. I imagine many people here lived like that before the war. But at least they had what was familiar upon which to stand and an opportunity to change if they could or if they chose, which is not possible when you lose everything,

It is ultimately about the human heart. I used to think it was about women. I used to think that only women were capable of expressing the compassion needed to change a world so full of hate but I was wrong. It is the human heart, exclusively the human heart that is capable of such a task.

Terenia encourages me to safeguard my confidence. She recommended this passage from the Bible: "So don't lose your confidence. It will bring you a great reward. You need endurance so that after you have done what God wants you to do, you can receive what he has promised." (Hebrews 10: 35-36.)

I am not interested in reward or recognition and I think our collective over culture has abused badly the notion of 'what God wants'. I am here to say, I'm not that clever to know what God wants.

What I do know is that life is damned hard and I don't deserve anything more than anyone else and what I do have I'd like to share with another.

I don't know if I ever told you about the old woman from the Muslim section of Istanbul. It's a story that forever shaped my life. I was never able to see life again in the same way after that. The old woman's grandson was my guide when I was twenty-five. I have no memory of why my partner decided to go off with the guide and leave me at the grandmother's house, but this is not important to the story.

I walked through the door of a concrete block. The floors were made of the same slab. There was a thin carpet laid down. There was a cot to the side of the wall and a small kitchenette. There were no chairs or tables. One made themselves comfortable on the floor. (God is good that He didn't offer me this experience today as I'm not sure how easily I could have gotten down to the floor nor how easily I could have returned to standing.) The old woman excused herself and went into the kitchen and re-emerged some ten minutes later with the most beautiful silver tea service I have ever seen. She proceeded to make me mint tea with all the gestures of one who'd been doing this her entire life. She offered me what you and I call Turkish Delights. Candies. Neither one of us spoke a word of each other's language. So we sat cross-legged on the floor and waited for the men to return, drinking our tea and eating our sweets. She shared with me the best of what she had and to this day, tears still well up in my eyes when I think of this story. That old woman changed my life. That someone so poor would offer so much. In my silly, ideological way, I guess this is the way I move through life, the way I want to be forever.

I love you Rose Kieniewicz and I miss you terribly. But I know you are looking down upon me and I know you are influencing my decisions.

I am forever grateful to you, my dear mother-in-law. My Naomi in the desert who always reminds me that God can take a hopeless situation and turn it into something miraculous.

P.S And you were right! I still can't speak but halting Polish. I'm not sure it will always be this way. I hope not. I have stacks of books and notebooks that fill at least two shelves of this blasted language ... they might yet find their way back to centre point in my life, but certainly not now.

> ... and that's what we do—we're all counters. We are! We think to ourselves, "You gave this much, so you deserve this much.
>
> Every such expectation is a resentment waiting to happen. When we expect, we're soon going to resent it when we don't get what we think we deserve. So, what the Gospel says is "Stop expecting!" Entitlement is lethal for the soul. Everything is a gift—one hundred percent pure gift. The reason any of us woke up this morning had very little to do with us and everything to do with God. All twenty-four hours today are total gift. And so, the only real prayer is to say "Thank you!" and to keep saying it. When our prayer is constantly "Thank you," and we know we deserve nothing, and that everything is a gift, we stop counting. Only when we stop counting and figuring out what we deserve, will we move from the world of merit into the wonderful world of grace. And in the world of grace, everything is free.
> Richard Rohr, 'Who Deserves Anything', homily September 21, 2014.

September 11, 2022
Day 200

This week, I am posting a letter written by the mother of one of our residents. This letter reminds me that war is not an Instagram post, not a 20 second soundbite or Facebook entry. I have not made corrections; it is as she sent it.

Meet Stepan, our son. He recently turned 13 years old. We haven't seen him for almost half a year, 180 long days and nights to be precise. On that horrible day, February 24, our life was changed forever. As for Stepan, it happened around noon of the same day when he saw planes and black helicopters flying, as it seemed, right at our house. They were on their way to bomb Hostomel while in our home in Bucha, as in some infernal theatre, we were watching this horrifying "play": a swarm of helicopters over Hostomel which is pretty close, machine gun bursts could be seen and heard, explosions, fire, downed helicopters falling to the ground and exploding. Seeing all of this, your consciousness refuses to accept it as real, happening here and now, in the nice and quiet Bucha, in the middle of Europe.

At first, he asked if we were going to die, why this was happening, why?! He was scared and stunned.

Stepan is special. He was born prematurely, with a brain hemorrhage. The doctors' forecasts were disappointing, but we fought desperately for him! Stepan has two brothers, and the whole family joined the difficult path of rehabilitation. Having a degree of a special education teacher, I decided to refresh my knowledge, as well as acquire new understanding. For his sake. With small and difficult steps, we won big victories, and those doctors' forecasts gradually lost their meaning! Yes, it wasn't easy to get rid of our problems, but Stepan himself understood what all this was for, and he also fought and ... won! And everything was going according to our plan, until suddenly WAR!

The world around us started to fall apart, and everything we built and gained for many years suddenly turned into ashes. What to do? It was unbearably painful and unclear. How to save years of hard but productive work, as well as the meaning of life. After all, Stepan's psyche which we rebuilt brick by brick might not last and crumble like a sand fortress.

With the whole family, we first went to the countryside, because it was dangerous to stay in Bucha, but we did not find peace there either. Things were flying above us and exploding, first in Zhytomyr, then on the Zhytomyr highway, then the Orks seized our nuclear plants and the threat of nuclear blackmail and occupation hung in the air.

We deliberated and decided to save the most vulnerable – we took Mom and Stepan across the Polish border on foot, handed them over to Polish volunteers. An hour later the child wrote to me that he had eaten, he was warm and everything was fine. My husband, our eldest son and I returned to Kyiv and joined a volunteer battalion, with the help of which we organized a humanitarian mission to evacuate families with children with disabilities (autism, cerebral palsy, epilepsy, Down syndrome and other developmental disorders) to institutions, specializing in or simply ready to accept such special refugees. After all, our own experience clearly highlighted the difficulties of getting such families to safety in conditions of panic and hopelessness! That's how I met Mr. Paul when I brought refugees from the Dnipro and Kyiv region.

Later, our battalion, which was accepted into the Armed Forces of Ukraine received a combat mission, and we went to the Donetsk region, where we are still serving.

Well, war is war, but the understanding that my mother and Stepan are safe is very warming and gives us strength and hope that soon all this will end, and we will be together again. We see how happy he is. He goes to school, has new friends, takes care of the little and special ones. He matured surprisingly quickly, and most importantly, all the problems that prevented him from living a full life simply receded, and maybe even disappeared. Forever. All the events and stress he experienced affected him, so he became strong and balanced. Stress can also have a positive result, so it happened in our case.

We miss him very much. So much. The child, for whom we fought for many years, was left without us. We see him growing up in videos and photos, but we do not see it with our own eyes. We cannot be close. It is very difficult for teenagers to be without the support of their parents at this period of their lives. We cannot bring him home to Bucha because it is not known how long the war will last, which means that we cannot be safe yet. We will be too far away, on the territory of one country, in which a very cruel war is going on with incredible an insidious enemy.

Our family is extremely grateful to all the people who are now helping other families fleeing the war. I don't know how to choose the words of gratitude – they will still not be enough, they will not be able to fully express all our feelings! Meanwhile, we will lead the war to victory, there can be no other way, and bring our long-awaited meeting closer.

P.S. Only Fate can destroy and reward at the same time. And only she can so aptly combine people's destinies at the right moment and in the right circumstances. Such a moment in my life was meeting Amber and Paul – people with a huge heart and an infinitely kind soul! I am happy for such a reward from Fate.

September 17, 2022
Day 206

> "There was more time then, and folk were fewer, so
> that most men were distinguished." (Farmer Giles
> of Ham: Tolkien)

It's been a busy week. The children have returned to school. The mornings are noticeably cooler, the leaves are turning to crimson and yellow, and no one could be happier than I to know that soon both fireplaces will emerge from their summer slumber, robust as ever. The season for bundling up is upon us. Gloves, hats, boots, slipper socks, hot chocolate and peppermint schnapps, winter birthdays and Christmas stockings stuffed with delight.

Some of our residents are working at the sewing factory in Staszów. It's hard work but they are protected by European labour laws, which is a relief to know they're not subject to the exploitation typical in such an industry. Paul has become acquainted with the owner of the shop and he likes her, which is another reason for relief. For those who can work and save their money, it's all the more beneficial to them once the war is over.

I am of two minds about the whole affair but must yield to the desires of those in residence. I am not opposed to hard work but I am always on the lookout for exploitive tendencies subtly disguised as "fair trade". It's not unusual for immigrants across the globe to agree to more than the local would agree to in hopes of a chance to belong in their desire to feel protected.

Human dignity. To be treated ethically. What does that mean? It's a slippery concept. Immanuel Kant considered value to be relative, because the value of something depends on the observer of such a value judged. According to Thomas E. Hill, Jr. (Emeritus Kenan Professor of Philosophy at the U. of North Carolina at Chapel Hill and a specialist in ethics, political philosophy, history of ethics and the work of Immanuel Kant) "... All persons, regardless of rank or social class, have an equal intrinsic worth or dignity. ...This moral law requires respect for human dignity because all human persons, good or bad, must, from the standpoint of practice, be presumed to have the capacities and predispositions of rational autonomy.

Paul waited at school with one of the mothers yesterday for a psychiatrist's arrival. He had been scheduled to meet with him about her son who is having difficulty adjusting to this new environment. M. was born prematurely resulting in an underdeveloped brain. He cannot walk or speak, feed or dress himself and he screams when he is distressed. I don't know why he shrieks but I would guess when the stimulus is more than he can make sense of this is how he reacts.

The doctor showed no emotion or compassion toward the boy or his mother. From a majority of doctors today, anywhere in the world, this is not a requirement nor is it something one can any longer expect. So that this doctor was without emotion is not unusual. What was unusual however is that he breached the line of human dignity. Had Paul not been there as advocate to this mother and child, they would have both walked away distraught. As it was, they were all fairly agitated when they left the school.

After much inquiry, Paul finally got out of the doctor exactly what the medicine prescribed was called. At first the doctor resisted, saying she, referring to the mother, could look it up online. No. Paul insisted this was not an acceptable practice of medicine. He reminded the doctor that he was the doctor and he needed to tell them what the name of the medicine was and if it had potential side effects of any kind. The doctor was not keen on Paul but did finally give him the information about the medicine. He also became a bit friendlier and said to try it for a week and see how it worked. When the mother asked, "Supposing he doesn't like it?" To which the doctor decried, "How would you know if he doesn't like it. He can't talk."

Let me be very clear here. There is no reason whatsoever to believe this doctor has any prejudice against Ukrainians. This is actually not about the Ukrainians but about us as human beings.

Perhaps he didn't cross a line at all. Perhaps it comes down to plain old empathy. The kind of stuff you learn when you learn to wash your hands and brush your teeth. To share your toys and to care when someone else is crying or hurt or sad.

One of the women I've met online since the war started is Karen who sent me a book title yesterday, *The Power of Kindness: Why Empathy is Essential in Everyday Life* by Brian Goldman, M.D. She talks about how the chapter titled, Teach Me, which, in part, she continues tells of the Roots of Empathy program offered to classes of Grade 4 children in Toronto. Then she goes on to say how it has helped "some children who are malnourished in the loving compassion department, how they see the world differently." In the forward of the book itself, Dr Goldman describes how he took his practice outside of the hospital and travelled the world to understand why some people are more inclined to empathy than others. Definitely a book I plan to order.

I could not have predicted the ways in which I have changed since living with those who have lost everything; in particular, a sharpened sensitivity to the impact of our words and our actions. For this I will be forever grateful. If you are awake, you will recognise your teachers. And each and every one of the Ukrainians living here in refuge is a teacher.

So I notice stories about the doctor. I'm on the lookout for the subtleties of human indignity in ways that I would not have been inclined before.

We live in a world where we are more and more desensitized. We're asked to absorb thousands and thousands of images every day. Soundbites. Stories of tragedy and global economic collapse create an atmosphere of panic. No wonder we have to teach empathy in our classrooms, read out loud the definition of human dignity. And put it at the top of the lunch menu: Compassion, for those who are malnourished in this department.

On Saturdays, I talk to our son, Zack, who lives in Denver. He said to me today. "You know Mom, what's the first thing a teenager does when he feels like he doesn't belong? He causes trouble to get noticed." We were talking about how vulnerable the teen years are and how imperative it is to create a space of belonging for them.

I don't always get it right in this situation. Sometimes I lose my temper because I'm one of those personalities prone to such. My nephew, Jordan, who lives with us, frequently reminds me to "respond, not react" but I don't get that right either. So I don't think it's about always getting it right. But what I do know is that I am willing to go the distance with another person. I'm willing to live with a mess until the mess clears up and I'm willing to commit to a brighter future for all of us.

September 26, 2022
Day 215

Thanks to our cousin Stefan Dunin-Wąsowicz, four of our residents are now working at the sewing factory in Staszow. Another two are working for a firm that produces hand-painted Christmas tree ornaments. Stefan also found jobs for two of the young men desperate to work since they arrived. Both boys are here in the capacity of helping their mothers and their families but do have the desire to do more, so gainful employment has been a welcomed relief.

Meanwhile, every morning we get a delivery of protective pads for Polish soldiers delivered to us. The women who are not working outside the house, have a job inside, packaging the pads so they can be sent out. Not only is this an opportunity to support the military who defend our borders against Russian aggression, but it is the perfect solution for those who are unable to find immediate employment, a chance to earn some money while they wait. We hope more such opportunities will show up.

None of our residents want to be in a situation of perpetual charity. The value of sheltering, providing basic needs and seeing to it that children are safely tucked up in school while the mothers work, allows them to accumulate resources to help them transition to a new life. It is a stroke of empowerment.

Where will that new life be? Ukrainians have strong cultural and family ties. Though Canada has opened its borders to Ukrainian refugees, Canada is half a world away. Its language and culture are foreign. It is a momentous decision to move that far away from one's cultural roots, not a decision that our residents are inclined to do. Staying in Poland and developing a life here is certainly an option, however rents in the cities are high and not many landowners want to rent to Ukrainians. Landowners worry that the tenants may up and leave for the Ukraine after a couple of months, or end up unable to afford the rent. Until a family has some savings, a move to the city, where admittedly jobs are more plentiful, is risky.

A return to the Ukraine is something seldom discussed given the current military situation. Most of our residents are from Kharkiv, Bucha, Dniepro or Zaporizhzhia. No one wants to live under the Russian rule. History is too painful. Many of our guests keep the flame of hope alive, small though it is, a hope that one day they will be able to reclaim their aborted lives.

We do what we can to help feed that flame.

October 23, 2022
Day 242

THE IMAGINATION OF THE CHILDREN

Edith Kramer says, 'Art tells the Truth'. 'The need to make art is a universal need.'

How does art fit in when the horror of war comes to roost in your country? Is art an indulgence, a waste of time when on the run from war?

We should ask Gala, who cares for the art gallery here at the Cross Border House.* With the loving kindness of an attentive mother, she is organised, focused, and creative. She inspires the children here to make art. She receives visiting teachers, artists, set designers and costumers from the U.K. and America, all of whom have visited during the past seven months to work with Gala and the children.

But Gala's presence provides something more. She is a child psychologist by profession. I have seen children who wouldn't look me in the eye seven months ago or who clung to their mothers for dear life transform into dynamic pods of vitality and free spirit, bounding with energy all because they have acclimated to the holistic care of their environment and Gala, who guides them daily in some form or other of activity. She encourages these children to express themselves through their art; to say what they can't say with words. Sometimes it's just holding one child in her lap while soothing their hurt feelings from any number of expected encounters on the playground. She brings her values and her art to those in trouble.

Art Therapist Edith Kramer studied under the mentorship of Friedl Dicker-Brandeis at the Bauhaus before the start of WWII. Kramer immigrated to America while there was still time to escape the Nazis but Friedl would suffer a different fate. Before she lost her life in the gas chamber at Auschwitz, she was an art teacher, illustrator of book covers, stage and costume designer and creator of children's toys. This is what she brought with her to Terezin. Literally. Instead of packing clothes, Friedl packed paper, paints, brushes and other art supplies. Of the 200,000 women and children from Terezin concentration camp, 15,000 were children. Of these 15,000 only 232 survived.

Before Friedl was transported to Auschwitz, she packed two suitcases filled with children's drawings. These drawings were discovered ten years later hidden away at Terezin. I saw this exhibition at the Pinka Synagogue in Prague some years ago.

Before I even knew my own destiny and what my own personal relationship to war would be, I was in great psychic turmoil over these drawings of underwater sea creatures, country roads leading to country cottages, a fairy princess shrouded in black being attacked by some kind of predator-like dragon, airing mattresses in the garden, a forest. Children's drawings by children who should have been at home in their own beds who instead were in a filthy camp, terrified, and hungry. Children whom I knew had died long ago.

We cannot compare this war to that war anymore than we can compare either of these wars to the Mongol conquests for instance or the Thirty Years War as another example. Each war has its own identity, its own brand of politics and aggression, its own type of violence and strategies.

War is who we are. We are war. There is no one morally spared from this truth.

But the question I asked was, is art an indulgence? Especially in times of war. Any war.

No. The answer is, it is not an indulgence.

In the case of the children of Terezin, perhaps for those few blessed opportunities they had to draw, they were able to use paper and paint to hoist them into a safe place, a place of forests and cottages houses to a back garden where children were busy playing.

The Cross Border House Gallery, in the spirit of someone like Brandeis or Kramer, serves to comfort these children in flight from war, who might have, under other conditions, faced a different fate. For the children here who have the freedom to express themselves through art, guided by a woman who is conscious of the importance of such activities for those who have been traumatised, we are most grateful.

My nephew, Jordan, also an artist, helps in the CBH Gallery. He said to me: 'Art is important. Expression is important. Exhibition is not. The commodification of art is not.'

The war rages on next door. With power outages, food and medicine shortages, no heat, and contaminated drinking water, the diaspora from Ukraine is certainly once again to be set in motion with its impact anticipated by its neighbouring borders from a new ground swell of refugees soon to cross.

*We have recently renamed our commitment to shelter the refugees running from war in Ukraine The Cross Border House. The community still resides on the property so graciously provided us by Stefan Dunin-Wasowicz.

November 6, 2022
Day 256

WAR

This month has been especially difficult and for no apparent reason; at least nothing I can identify in plain terms as the cause. No one is sick. No one is making unreasonable demands. Apart from a few emotional outbreaks among us, the atmosphere seems amiable enough. So why am I flat? What is this weight upon me that disturbs my joy? If it is no one occurrence that I can point to, then perhaps it is a sequence of endless ones that I must bring together in order to understand this despondency.

War, shelter, home, at home, children, estranged, fathers, brothers, soldiers, killers, rape: despair.

The End and the Beginning
by Wisława Szymborska

After every war
Someone has to clean up.
Things won't
Straighten themselves up, after all.

Someone has to push the rubble
To the side of the road,
So the corpse-filled wagons
Can pass.

Someone has to get mired
In scum and ashes,

Sofa springs,
Splintered glass,
And bloody rags.

Someone has to drag in a girder
To prop up a wall.
Someone has to glaze a window,
Rehang a door.

Photogenic it's not,
And takes years.
All the cameras have left
For another war.

The definition of the word shelter: something beneath, behind or within which a person, animal or thing is protected from storms, missiles or adverse conditions; refuge.

The definition of 'at home': in one's own house or place of residence, in one's own town or country, prepared or willing to receive social visits, in a situation familiar to one at ease.

Factory work in the dining area. Lunch prepared by the community. Delicious, sometimes even more than delicious; superb. Children playing, bickering, playing, crying, laughing. Dogs barking. Grown-ups at the table talking about the future in hopeless terms. "I see no hope in the future," they say, then slip back into their quarters. The glass cover on my phone is all cracked up, splitting apart. I have resisted having it repaired because it seems the perfect metaphor.

Anxiety: Winter is coming. We are depending on blankets and firewood; saving the gas for colder weather.

I am only a witness to war, not a victim. My choice has been a choice of solidarity, nothing more. Otherwise, I am spoiled and privileged but for the presence of war.

I went to a wedding mid-October and saw our first cousin, Janek, who lived at Ruszcza (Paul's parents' house) during THE WAR. Jan was only four but he remembers those days. He made a speech over the bride and groom and it reminded me of the one that his grandfather Antoni Kieniewicz made in June, 1939 above the heads of Rose and Henry. I told him about this speech and that I have it ... someplace. As the son of Poland's National Historian, he would like to include it in the family archives. I promised to send it to him. It was a speech full of hope and promise. And then there was war, the newlyweds, compelled to be apart for six years.

Two weeks later he called to say his wife of 60 plus years had died. Paul went to the funeral and said that Janek managed to stand before the attendees though didn't say much except a resounding, 'Do zobaczenia, Grazyna!' which means, 'See you soon, Grazyna.'

Looking for joy at a wedding and a funeral.

WAR.

Our cousin, Basia, came to stay with me while Paul was away in London visiting family. Basia is more like a sister to me than a cousin. She brought with her the letters her mother and father had written to her grandmother back in Poland after the war.

Jan Rostworowski married Teresa Horodynska in Edinburgh in 1945 after their lives, restricted by war, obliged them to settle in Great Britain. To return to a Russian occupied country, after having lived abroad would have increased the risk of imprisonment even a possible exile to Siberia. Her mother had already spent over 2 years of the war in a Soviet labour camp and had no desire to return.

We sat down at the computer together and Basia translated the letters from Polish into English as she read. She explained that the letters were in code. For example, instead of writing, Dear Mama, it was Dear Aunt so as not to bring to the attention of the communist authorities the fact that his mother had a son in the UK. The communists wouldn't have been as interested in interrogating her over a distant relative.

The aftermath of war and the way one must change their lives to fit in.

The longing they felt, filtered through the lines in each letter. They were lonely. They had a hard time with the language and with making friends in Britain. It was cold and damp. But they worked and they worked hard. Jan had to delay his dreams of poetry, of writing, for another ten years. Teresa managed the children and worked eight to ten hours a day at a desk job. They missed being at home.

There is a certain sound, a kind of music that the landscape of one's own home imparts. There is a fragrance there too. Attached to this is a visual image of the colours and the light and the shadows. There is all of this in the origin of one's own home. Everything else is merely a shelter. A substitute.

As Basia read the letters, I wept. The tears are so close to the surface these days. Though how can one not weep at the unnatural and aggressive force used to divide a citizen from his country of origin?

War and After the War. The glass is cracked.

The letters go on to describe their lives, sometimes communicating quite joyful moments with the children but always aware they cannot return to Poland. They are political exiles with refugee papers. Under such circumstances, their only means of communication were their letters to Jan's mama.

After a decade, Jan did finally find the time and creative space to write. He joined the Polish expatriate community of artists and writers and was celebrated for his work. But it was not to last. He was rejected by them, his name and his work smeared when in the mid-sixties he made the decision to take a Polish passport, (his application for British citizenship was rejected), and return to Poland for the first time to see his mother. He was vilified as a traitor to the cause by accepting the document from the government of the Polish People's Republic.

Jung said that '...when an inner situation is not made conscious, it happens outside, as Fate.'

But how much control do we have as individuals over the collective and what It does not make conscious? I say our destinies are restricted at best, shattered at worst and left forever stunted, unable to reclaim the strength it would take to redefine an individual plan secure enough to support a destiny. This is the reality of circumstance of which none of us are exempt.

I tire of trying to make sense of war, either spiritually, rationally, or theoretically or otherwise; I must carry the burden of when my faith fails. I don't expect to understand the mystery of God. I don't even look for certainty. Not all the time, anyway. So when I say faith, it's not faith in my relationship with God that I doubt or that is called into question. It is this discontent within with which I struggle. My greatest joy is to be in service but I feel no joy. My enthusiasm has leeched out of me.

My son, Zack, wrote to me today, referencing the photographs of Paul's ancestors hanging here at Sichów and at Kurozwęki.

He writes:

> All the pictures are amazing, but do you actually think for one second that those ancestors had it easy? They are pretty and restored and in black and white ... you can't see them in color. You don't see the typhoid and cholera, dysentery and rheumatic fever. You don't see the three children out of eight that didn't make it or live long enough for a photograph. There wasn't any EU or ERCC to offer any assistance in a drought or pandemic, flu or famine. Fall off a horse and break your leg 20 miles from civilization with no back up, you still have to climb back on and get home. You don't see this in the photographs, but it's there in living colour. They had hard lives yet celebrated the fine moments of happiness in between because they were strong ...

I must add to his observations our own family heritage from West Texas at the turn of the 19th to the 20th Century when his great grandparents settled a cattle ranch with their eleven children. I remember my aunts talking about the Native Americans and the challenges they faced.

It would be unnatural to feel joy while partnering those whose lives have been forever changed by war. What joy is there in that? Neither should one expect joy from service. Service is a neutral activity. It must have no name to be authentic. When service is bound up and identified with the one in attendance to the other, then it becomes more about the individual than it does about the service.

I am finding my way back again after many weeks of melancholy. And why shouldn't my heart break? What else is the heart supposed to do?

Jordan says it breaks so that it can grow again even stronger.

WAR.

The next time there is a national holiday with flags flying and parks full of patriotic exuberance, just remember that somewhere in the world there is a population of people who suffer until the end of their days the impact of war. War does not make us free. There is always another one waiting in the wings in which to enlist. What makes us free is within us.

November 6, 2022
Day 276

This is a War Diary entry. I am tired of counting the days. Counting the days toward what, I wonder. Toward resolution, toward peace, toward kindness, toward tolerance, toward what? The end of a brutal war? A new civilization?

> 'Ukrainian officials said Wednesday that overnight airstrikes by Russian forces hit a hospital maternity ward in southern Ukraine, killing a newborn baby and wounding its mother.' November 23, 2022.

I wasn't yet thirty when I visited the Prado in Madrid and saw Picasso's iconic *Guernica*. I didn't know it at the time, but it had just been returned to Spain under heavy guard from the MOMA in New York. I was young and unaware of what I gazed upon, in spite of an erudite guide who took us through each section of this massive mural-like painting structured like a modern triptych.

What did Bernard Shaw say? Something about youth being wasted on the young?

There was no victory in this painting. 1,645 people were killed on that market day morning; mostly women and children. Their men were fighting elsewhere. It was at the height of the Spanish Civil War that this bombardment by German and Italian allies of General Franco took place.

I remembered something very vivid from the painting. A woman with a dead child in the upper left hand corner. The guide pointed to this section of the painting, indicating its resemblance to the Pieta. Our

Lady. Mater Dolorosa. Our Lady of Sorrows, most often portrayed with multiple swords piercing the heart.

I consider the fate of the woman unprotected. The child encased in the holy waters of the womb seems the only place of safety. While it lasts. Society suffers from an absence of feeling which breeds alienation and apathy. In such an atmosphere, both woman and child are exposed to the threat of massacre, especially those in poverty and situations compromised by aggression, war, and political barbarity. The mother and child as objects are then conspicuously faceless, expendable, deadwood, excess baggage, non-essentials. One can do with them what they please.

I just stepped away from my desk for a moment and walked past one of the rooms where a woman was heaving tears. At first, it sounded like exuberant laughter, but as I listened more carefully, in fact, it was the pain of war that I heard. She is separated from what is familiar.

We all live here together amongst broken dreams and shattered lives. The brute shock of war that is unrelenting. Trapped between despair and doubt we do our best to get through each day.

Last night at the table, our Friday gathering with wine and nuts, like a real life when people are free to move about and visit friends after a long week of work, when they have someplace to go - we sit at this table and pretend that we have normal lives too, even if it's just for a few minutes over a glass of wine and a shared story.

The apartment blocks in Kharkiv rise to sixteen stories, someone offered. They have to take the stairs. No refrigeration. No lights, food shortages and people drinking water from the rivers. A story was told about a man who sold the contents of his freezer for money.

I'm sure I didn't understand it as the story makes no sense to me this morning.

Hope is such a fragile assumption. There's no place to grip. Perhaps we should just capitulate to war strategies and a dictator, trying to make a mother believe he cares for the son he has just murdered. How have we become so deluded? Maybe from a century of literal bombardment have we grown weary and indifferent.

In an article by Rabbi Jeffrey Newman,* he quotes from Jonathan Lear's book, *Radical Hope:* 'When the buffalo went away, the hearts of my people fell to the ground ... and they could not lift them up again. After this, nothing happened.'

Rabbi Newman goes on to say, 'It is precisely this point – a people faced with the end of their way of life prompts the psychological, philosophical and ethical inquiry pursued in *Radical Hope.* How can we face the possibility that our culture or even our civilization might collapse?'

I'm intrigued by Newman's words, 'After this, nothing happened.' What does that mean? 'After this' might mean they were no longer able to reinvent themselves as a tribe. To reorganise or to even re-enchant their lives. Hope.

I try not to expect too much from the day. I am not in control. I make an effort to be in the kitchen when the soup is being served, as it runs out quickly. I do not want to disappear into inaction, so I write. And now, with the first snow, I think I will work on my new fairy tale and see how far I get.

---

* Jeffrey Newman is Emeritus Rabbi of Finchley Reform Synagogue. Plenty Coups. The last great Chief of the Crow Nations (1848-1932)

'My whole life as an artist has been nothing more than a continuous struggle against reaction and the death of art. In the picture, I am painting – which I shall call Gurenica – I am expressing my horror at the military caste which is now plundering Spain into an ocean of misery and death.' Pablo Picasso

1937. 2022. We are the same violent creatures.

Here are some words by Susan Winokur Platt whose grandmother immigrated from Ukraine to America in 1900.

Immigrant
by Susan Winokur Platt

There were people there. Thousands and thousands of people.
They were there for hundreds of years, although none of those years were easy.
They knew cold, they knew hunger, they knew poverty. Dirt floors.
But that is where they lived. And they did the best they could.
Eeking out a living, to feed their families.

Selling things.
Trading things.
A dollar here.
A dollar there.
They knew they were hated,
They knew it didn't make sense.

Cheerfully getting water from the well, my great grandfather was shot in the back.
And then they were all murdered.
By the thousands.
And thousands.
And thousands
Right in their own towns, their own villages.
They were forced to dig their own graves.
They killed everyone.
Mothers.
Fathers.
Toddlers.
Babies.
And it wasn't the first time.
My grandmother would say "Don't say 'ick' about food"
My grandmother would say "You should eat. I would have been glad to have that."
My grandmother would say "You don't let a pan soak! You use elbow grease!"
My grandfather, paralyzed from a stroke, would say
"Do you want something to eat?" and hand me a dollar.
I would then return that dollar to my grandmother, waiting for it in the kitchen,
And she would return it to his pants pocket,
After he went to bed.
I got the same dollar hundreds of times.
I do know about the hate.
When a boy called me a "kike" in the 7th grade,
I didn't know what the word meant.
My brother had to explain.
The decision to leave

Because they knew
What was happening,
What was coming.
Hoping for better.
They did that for our family, not really knowing
How, or even if,
It would turn out.
And now, two hundred, one hundred, or maybe,
Only sixty years later,
Here I am.
Never hungry. Never poor. Never cold.
So grateful to be an immigrant.

December 4, 2022

> "The legacy and horror of exile are ever with us."
> Stephan Hoeller

Father Richard Rohr reminds us that we don't need to know; that certitude is a misconception. Stephan Hoeller writes, "The monotheistic religions, Judaism, Christianity, and Islam, in their mainstream manifestations have placed much emphasis on faith. "I believe" (credo) is the central affirmation of much of the conventional religious mind...not faith, but a certain interior knowing liberates one from unconsciousness and eventually transports one beyond the bounds of manifest existence itself."

What is this yearning in man to know, to know for certain?

Is this a phenomenon among only 'believers' or is this universal to each of us? Is this anxiety only present in those of faith? Is it faith that settles the insecurity or is it something else?

It's my experience that there is a big difference between knowing for certain, such as what the future holds and then the knowing, the inner knowing that originates from within, the knowing that defines us.

In 1959, John Freeman of the BBC interviewed Dr Jung about his life. When he was asked, "Do you believe in God?", Jung replied: "Difficult to answer. I know. I don't need to believe. I know."

When you know then you don't have to believe. You needn't have faith because in the inner knowing, there is a trust, not a faith that abides but a confidence much different than the need to know for certain. The need for proof or assurance: certitude.

Much like the woman who haemorrhaged without stopping, the story told in the Gospel of Mark, for which the question arises: was her action one of a last unconscious attempt at health when she touched the hem of The Lord's garment or can it be seen as something else, an inner knowing perhaps? "If I but touch his clothes, I will be made well", (Mark 5:28) A knowing that released her from sickness, a knowing that compelled Jesus to speak so forthrightly: 'Daughter, your faith has made you well; go in peace, and be healed of your disease." This is a very powerful statement: Your faith has made you well. He never touched her, but she touched Him. Or rather the hem of his garment. She did not need his touch nor his gaze for healing. So what was this confidence in her that bespoke an inner knowing in the words: "If I but touch his clothes ..." It was no ordinary faith. The deep humility and trust is evidenced by the Lord Himself who proclaims: "...your faith has made you well ...

Faith and inner knowing. Father Rohr says we don't need to know, in terms of certainty. And he's absolutely right. For what is this demand for certainty? How have we grown so dependent upon the need for predictability? This is one question I pose to myself during this Advent season as I prepare my heart for Christmas. But deeper still, as I prepare myself for the remainder of my days. What is this demand for certainty? And what does it mean to be a refugee? Questions when explored at their root, would each indicate a need for belonging.

With a world devoid of living mythologies, fairy tales and story, we have grown remarkably dull by an all-consuming tendency toward rational thinking. "If this, then that" kind of approach to living. Thinking in square meters as I call it. It limits. It's agonizing and it leads us away from our true nature. It also stultifies spontaneity, one of the greatest markers of synchronicity.

There is the moment of decision to fall off the cliff and there is that liminal space between the decision to do so and the actual fall. Is this faith? Trust, most assuredly. But we've grown so rational in our ways and in our habits, that we're afraid to fall off the cliff into our own inner knowing. We cling to a superficial faith, one supported by a tidy and carefully laid out plan for our future which repeatedly disappoints and sometimes even terrifies. I know because I do this. And if I do it, so do others.

How do we make our way to a living, inner knowing, where every day we strengthen our trust in that which is before us, larger than us? To like or prefer an outcome or end result, moreover, to expect one is magical thinking. In fairy tales, it is laid upon the hero/heroine of the story to complete a task. And this task is never possible to achieve alone. This task is intended to be so difficult and insurmountable that it's unavoidable the need to ask for help. The path is thorny and complicated, treacherous and deceptive. Clearly our protagonist rests on a knife edge.

But then pumpkins turn into carriages and mice into coachmen and glass slippers and dwarfs and poisoned apples and wickedness abound. The world of story erupts, thrusting us into chaos, capturing our imagination, cheering us all on to our own inner hero, our own inner knowing.

Refugees and Trust

These past few months have been especially distressing in ways that I never saw coming. On more than one occasion, I have cursed this war and its perpetrators. I have even gone to the very limit of asking those banal and foolish questions: "Why me? Why am I suffering so? Why is this happening?" Silence. As Krishnamurti would say: "You're asking the wrong question."

Grace, my helper, the tremendous, loving kindness of the presence of those beings in the spiritual world, my guardians, lead me into a deeper inner knowing and one that recognizes this status of being a refugee which is really, ultimately, all of us. To trust the path toward home again. To know, an inner knowing that we belong to something bigger, more vast, eternal and cosmic.

If we find a home within ourselves, can we be anywhere, living under any circumstance? Can we somehow access the inner knowing of St. Paul who knew that nothing can separate us from God's love even in the middle of the most fiendish storm?

It doesn't always feel like love though; amidst estrangement, war, aggression, loss of everything, deceit, betrayal, disappointment. But we have an assignment. As our global demography is increasingly challenged by the forced migration of people running from war, civil unrest due to food shortages and contaminated water and climate anomalies, it is imperative for those of us in a more privileged and settled situation to steel ourselves in trust to a greater presence, to train ourselves in compassion and be available in service to those in need. We have to start helping each other. We have to be the one who changes, the one who accepts God's promises in spite of the world indicating otherwise.

The task here at The Cross Border House is to continue to support each other and to co-create an atmosphere of love, tolerance and acceptance.

The children are downstairs painting Christmas tree ornaments and making origami lanterns. Light and beauty. Gala and Jordan spear head this project. Yulia is taking pictures, and all are in high spirits. They, too, are preparing. In this case, for the coming of the tree.

There are so many things I wish to share; the most significant is a letter that only recently surfaced written by Paul's Uncle Jan who wrote it upon hearing the death of Paul's grandmother in 1942. She died in Wójcza, thirty minutes from here. He wrote a detailed account of his journey by train and carriage, the surroundings and then a detailed portrait of this childhood wonderland and all its inhabitants, including Paul's mother. A time gone by.

He was a refugee of WWII, separated from his family in Poland until the last decade of his life.

From the "The Letter", by Jan Rostworowski.

"The House"

On the right of the house a rough tree trunk
leans,
Almost merging with the wall. A huge lime tree
One bough hangs low and on it we children.
Under the watchful eye of the terrified nanny,
Would swing heavenwards, so we named it
the cradle
So close were we then to heaven,
Closer than an adult who keeps asking

What undiscovered power is to be found up
above.
Until finally he is enlightened,
That it is in children that the answer to the
riddle can be found.

Jan Rostworowski, 1942

December 19, 2022

Dear Diary,

I have become bored with my own philosophy. It tires me out. A fresh start to the New Year looks more like vignettes. Not that these pages will be completely spared my introspection, but a considerable reprieve is in order. (I'm not that tired of hearing myself think.) What strikes me these days is to keep close to something the renowned mythologist Joseph Campbell said: 'We must be willing to let go of the life we planned, so as to have the life that is waiting for us.'

* * *

It's been nearly two weeks since Paul and I've had a chance to sleep in. We're up around 6:30 in the morning drinking coffee, bathing, dressing, and now, in addition, layering up to de-ice the car. It's snowing outside and has been for a century. At least, that's how one born to a Caribbean Island regards such weather. From my bedroom window, in bed, covered up, snuggled against a hot water bottle is how I enjoy the snow. Others have their own way; they actually like to go out in it. As my husband says, 'For those who like that sort of thing, that's the sort of thing they like.' (Spoiler: Pinched from *The Prime of Miss Jean Brodie*.)

We get up to make doctor's appointments. But before you judge us harshly, bear in mind that every country has their own shadow, that this is our personal peculiarity, our very own special attraction. One must stand in line before eight o'clock in the morning. Outside the clinic. Sometimes they open the door before eight and let you huddle up in the entryway like cattle, sometimes they don't. That's the easy part as you've yet to encounter Lady Cerberus, another special attraction. She guards the door with an admirable intensity. After shivering half to death in the snow, gaining entrance is a hospitality one cannot underestimate. As my mother used to say, 'Don't look a gift horse in the mouth.' By the time you reach your destination, you simply know it's going to go all wrong. It's not just that my Polish is abominable, as there are days when I go in alone, heaven help, and must navigate the territory like Hercules, but it's this way for everyone. There is no discrimination. First, there is the look of surprise at your presence, as if you've come to buy shoes instead of to see the doctor. Once established that you are there to make an appointment, then comes the insurmountable affair of finding the patient in the computer. No one is ever in that computer. No one. I think she's looking at a television screen, watching re-runs of *Stawka Większa Niż Życie* ... never mind. Then there's the scramble of her assistant as she rummages through filing cabinets dating back to 1960, containing written information on each of us. But it's never easy. It's never a situation of opening the drawer and then effortlessly retrieving what's needed. It's always a drama and lots of talk as I'm standing there, my body bent sideways at the waist because Cerberus sits behind bullet-proof glass with only about a foot of it open at the bottom.

Then comes the pronouncement. 'This name is not in the computer.'

The stare.

Please. This man is very sick and needs to see the doctor.

After a moment's consideration, a stronger stare, and quick movement of the hand as she slides something toward me under the small opening in the window, the verdict is in.

You will need to take these forms and fill them out before coming back. (Thank you. I didn't mention that I've filled out those forms twice before.)

Success. We have an appointment! It's been a journey, but someone had to do it.

The clock strikes 9:00.

* * *

The good bakery is around the corner, and if I'm not too late, there will still be fresh rolls. Doesn't that just evoke memories of a sidewalk cafe in Paris? A single croissant and coffee, a baguette held back for later. Lamentably, I've acquired a reputation in these villages that's a far cry from romantic. If you happen to be standing in line behind me, you will have to reconsider your options, as I will buy a variety of forty rolls each, plus an interesting assortment of sliced breads, plus, what Paul and I call 'Kitty Kat' bread. Plain white. By the time I load up, the baker is happy, but the customers are frustrated as their choices are reduced to crumbs.

A few nights ago, I was having trouble sleeping. Clearly, Paul was not. It was about ten o'clock and there was a knock at the door. It was Jordan returning my car keys from when he needed them earlier in the day. I went back to bed. Not long later, one dog threw up which woke up the other two. I cleaned up, settled our girl, and then turned off the light again. There was a knock at the door. I turned on the light. It was Jordan who needed the keys again. He must have left something in the car. I turned off the light and went back to bed. Not but minutes later Paul turns on the light, leaps out of bed to announce he's had a dream and where the hell is a pen. What a racket. Now the dogs are awake, and I'm sure he's sleep walking. I bought you four new pens today. Well, I can't find them. They're on your desk. No they're not. So, I get out of bed.

Of course, they're on his desk, but when I hand him one, he says it's too late; he's already forgotten the dream. Off goes the light. Finally.

It turns out the dream was about Wójcza, Paul's mother's home before the war. He could only remember that much, but not a narrative.

At wine night last night, I told this story with the help of my phone, my broken Polish, and a lot of gesturing, when to my surprise, someone said they'd had a dream too, on that same night, about God, Kharkiv, the war and an empty suitcase. Apparently, God said the suitcase wasn't important anymore.

There was a silence, as there often is when the war is mentioned. There's no heat or electricity there. No internet.

One of the little boys came in crying. I have no idea why.

Then we sang "Jingle Bells." I sang to the top of my lungs in English and the other women sang in Ukrainian.

* * *

The fruit is disappearing at an alarming rate, which seems strange because we've not had that problem before. And come to think of it, so are the shopping bags which we keep hanging inside the pantry door. Why is it that every time I reach for them, they've disappeared too.

The other night, while I was making eggs or sandwiches or something of the kind, I stepped out of the kitchen and there were the boys. The little boys. A whole gang of them. Each had a hulking shopping bag, and each were shovelling apples, mandarins and pears into the bag as fast as they could to my repressed, but clearly audible, gasp. They looked up, shovelled another scoop before tearing down the hallway like Fagin's band of thieves.

One the one hand, it was a precious sight and did evoke memories of old English literature and wintery nights sitting in front of the fireplace while Paul would read to me. Yes, we do this. We always spend our winters reading books to each other. He read the entire Lord of the Rings to me before we married.

On the other hand, I felt a sudden loss of control. An instability which was completely irrational but still felt like I was on the border between manageability and outright inner turmoil.

* * *

Christmas in a kitchen with about twenty women on the committee to decide what gets cooked and by whom. Three intersecting cultures, one space, of which there is actually no space large enough to hold twenty women with twenty different ideas about what should be laid on the Christmas table.

I think this vignette is worth a later short story. Certainly, there will be much more to report as we get through this week. Even as I write, one woman comes with the list. Two others come to ask me not to order the fish too early because of another woman in the house who will take it to her room and put it in the window for herself to cook later. (It's in minus degrees outside so this is possible.)

* * *

At the meeting this morning to decide about the children's presents and some symbolic gift for the adults to open, our dear Masha came running to her mother to say that her godmother was safe in Kharkiv. She had been on their minds almost constantly these past few weeks when she escaped the occupied territories, as her home had been destroyed and everything in it and was now homeless, moving west without a plan. Masha decided to write to the headmaster of her high school and see if there was any work at all for her godmother and a place for her to stay. He wrote her back and said to tell her godmother to come and they would take care of her.

There is no electricity except what is produced from independent generators. Lessons have been interrupted for the unforeseen future.

This war is ugly, dangerous and destructive. It's a real war and people are dying. They are starving and they're going without heat. This is real.

It's very hard for me to raise a toast to life when just hours away this is happening. It's irreconcilable.

* * *

Christmas is almost here. We always keep an empty chair at the table for a stranger who might come calling.

I think of this chair as a place for me to grow my compassion even greater. What will finally put an end to these hellish wars? Some would argue nothing because we've always had war. But I counter argue that greater compassion, deliberate tolerance, and resolve to serve another in need will at least affect a positive change and that change can only happen one by one. One person must make the inner commitment to do this. Not for one's own personal happiness do we make this resolution. What the hell is that anyway when the world is on fire?

P.S. Dear Diary,
I keep thinking I'll finish this entry before too much else happens but the mayor of Staszow just called to say there is a Ukrainian teenager without a home over the holidays. He is apparently in a residential situation but with no place to go over the Christmas/New Year's break. We have absolutely no private rooms left, but we are going to make a place for him in front of the upstairs fireplace. We will hang sheets to give him some privacy. At least he will be warm and there is a downstairs bathroom which is quite accessible.

December 25, 2022

Christmas at The Cross Border House
December, 2022

I made too many lasagnes. Three too many to be exact. I could have stopped with the three I made on the Thursday ahead of Christmas Day and spared myself the outburst on Friday when I approached the kitchen assuming I'd have a square meter of space in which to work, even willing to settle for half that, when there she was, the cause of my misery, spread out over the entire kitchen. There wasn't room enough to pour a glass of milk; each countertop had been taken over by her mass production of fried breads stuffed with leftover potatoes. (Honestly, it's as if she's anticipating the Polish Army to sally through on their way to the border.) And two days before Christmas.

I stormed out of the kitchen. I wrote to a dear friend of mine that very same day, damning the whole affair. "She reminds me of that nursery rhyme about the magic porridge pot that would yield its porridge only upon the command 'little pot boil' and finish when you said, 'little pot stop.' But if you forgot how to stop it, as was the moral and point of the nursery rhyme, when the little girl forgot the witch's instructions, porridge overflowed from the pot, filling up the house, spilling out of the windows into the street in an endless, unstoppable stream throughout the town and into the villages."

Where was my Christmas spirit? There were many things on my list I'd yet to strike off. There was the Apteka. I needed to buy enough children's medicines to see us through the holidays. We needed extra blankets and towels. We needed soap, toothpaste, basic hygienic items in case families coming from Ukraine needed anything. I could run those errands while waiting for space in the kitchen. I didn't need to put myself on show like that just because I didn't get my way

Twenty-two women in a kitchen. Is that the equivalent of how many angels can dance on the head of pin? Maybe not. Let's not exaggerate our optimism.

If one is prepared for the psychological impact of living within a community of those whom you know not, then marvellous discoveries about yourself are likely.

The honest truth about 'my misery' is she's actually a lot like me. Or at least like I was. She has a son who is very sick. At one time, my son was also very sick and at risk of dying. She feels alone. She's a big personality. She feeds people. It's a feeding instinct that sets up in the body either from a lack of one's own sufficient emotional nourishment in childhood or from years of scarcity. It can manifest as the devouring mother, but I simply call it 'the feeder.'

As I said, I can see her in my reflection. I remember carrying what she carries. This softens me to her and helps me not judge her so harshly.

(P.S. She does make the most amazing pastries filled with a kind of farmers cheese and just a hint of raisins or currants that are lightly fried in oil which are truly out of this world!)

Wigilia (Polish Christmas Eve) welcomed a table of twelve fish dishes and salads galore ... plus fried bread stuffed with leftover potatoes. Paul explained the Polish tradition of sharing Opłatek, which began with thin wafers blessed by the priest. Each person receives their own wafer. As we approach each other, we break the wafer and express our good wishes as we pass the piece to them to eat. This is our ritual before sitting down to the table. What struck me was how unreserved we all were in our personal greetings as we all wished each other love. It was truly extraordinary. Not an experience I've ever had before. A feeling of tremendous love among people I didn't really know very well despite living together for nearly a year.

After Opłatek, confusion ensued because in Ukraine one starts with compote and kutia. Compote is a warm blend of dried fruits and brandy. Kutia is made from poppy seeds and honey. It's all so delicious but the Poles start with Barszcz, beetroot soup with uszka (tiny dumplings). We managed to combine these two cultural traditions without too much fuss.

Christmas Day. Too many lasagnes. Chicken, potatoes and all things leftover from Christmas Eve. Another feast of sharing stories and lots and lots of laughter.

January 12, 2023
Happy New Year

The skies have been grey since memory allows. The weather was much more appealing when it snowed for days on end, then abated, then snowed some more. The weather and its nature were doing what they do in winter, or at least how it used to be in Central Poland. There was a time when four seasons could be identified by an exact date, almost like the flip of a switch. The celebrations of the winter solstice, decorating the tree, of holly and mistletoe and the lighting of the candles all made more sense in the snow. Is that really the point though? Am I so distressed about the weather, or is it something else?

The once-expected cycles of nature are no longer predictable, thus here I sit beneath grey skies/warm weather. The weather is changing. This is a fact. More to the point, the climate is changing, but so seems to me the climate of the collective. This is my uneasiness. These are my questions.

Are we more ethical than we were 200 years ago? We were slaveowners. Women had no rights. Children under ten worked in factories without health or safety measures in place. This must be the wrong question as clearly, we were not.

A young philosopher William MacAskill, who has coined a new word: "long-termism", suggests humanity has the moral responsibility to protect the future. This philosophy more closely defines what bothers me. In an interview on NPR from his book *What We Owe the Future*, he says: "If you're thinking about the possibility of harming someone, [it doesn't] really matter if that person will be harmed next week or next year, or even in a hundred or a thousand years. Harm is harm."

We know when we hurt someone close to us that we must apologise, but how do we reconcile the unintentional harm we cause; the harm we cause from inaction or sheer helplessness? We know the reprehensible conditions under which the cobalt is extracted from the mines for our cell phones yet we continue to buy them. It somewhat reminds me of the young man who reproached Krishnamurti once for wearing leather shoes when K. turned to him and in a sharp tone said, "Sir. Make sure yours is the minimum". I don't know how to stop the artisanal mining in the Congo. If I thought that my puny contribution of not buying a cell phone would help, then I'd do it, but we all know the futility of such an action. If, say, 90% put down their phones, then this would be a game changer.

So what's my point? The refugees are in our house, at least the house that we lease. It's not our house, which causes me great concern because ultimately, this security too shall be taken away.

How long is too long to care for refugees? What determines the level of care extended to them? Who sets the standard? Why are they at risk of exploitation?

If one looks deeply at the word 'long-termism', would we make the same decisions? George Bernard Shaw felt that if man lived 300 years or more, he would be more inclined to make decisions favourable to the collective and not just for himself out of self-interest.

According to IDMC (Internal Displacement Monitoring Centre) there are 59.1 million internally displaced people in the world. 53.2m by conflict and violence and 5.9m by disasters. Forty are living here. What is my responsibility to their great-grandchildren's future? Do I have a responsibility to the unborn?

I did not go out seeking this situation. It knocked on my door and now that the situation is in the house that I lease, it is definitely, unequivocally my responsibility to do everything I can to support, partner and honour those souls who have crossed this threshold. It is my responsibility to act in their best interest, not in my self-interest.

There are a lot of ideas about how one should 'handle' the refugee crisis. Some ideas resonate with me, like the careful transitional programs which protect mother and child, wisely relocating them, when necessary, from one place to another of equal or greater care. Most are tossed out when the host gets tired of them or can't afford them or are annoyed by them due to personality clashes. The risk of exploitation is now thinly disguised, the longer the crisis continues. We simply don't have enough sustainable programs in place for this transition to occur humanely.

I am also in favour of greater autonomy, but, here again, this takes patience and a careful plan forward if one is thinking in terms of the future, and not just today's future but perhaps even hundreds of years into the next century.

Finally, I'm not sure why I'm thinking about this particular children's story today, one that I read to Zachary over and over again when he was a boy, but I am and this is one of the things I remember. When the Skin Horse talks to the rabbit about being real: "Real isn't how you are made," said the Skin Horse. "It's a thing that happens to you. When a child loves you for a long, long time, not just to play with but really loves you, then you become real." *The Velveteen Rabbit.*

Maybe because my experience in service to people who are displaced and without a home, a true home, not one that can be taken away again at any moment, that this reality has made me a better person. In so many ways it has made me real, the love that flows through me for them and the love that flows through them for me.

January 29, 2023
Day 340

Approaching the *War Diaries* from a distance, I'm always so sure about what I'm going to say until I get right up to the typewriter (so to speak). And then it changes. Remember those days? As my husband will tell you, before computers there were fewer who dared the undertaking of such a craft. Carbon paper had to be considered. Onion skin paper. Pencils, erasers, white out. Messy ribbons, red and black. The slow pace of the craft itself, producing the best we had to offer; then the swell and agony of the submission/ rejection process, the hope and the fall which left us in tears. If you were lucky, an editor would scratch some directional notes on the enclosed letter of refusal leaving you in a state of watchful euphoria as you bragged to all your friends: "They didn't accept my work but at least they told me the reasons why." It wasn't read by a robot or a twenty-two-year-old who'd never known anything but hyper-abundance and indulgence. Of course at the time, we didn't realise how precious were our blessings.

Henry Miller lived off Beverly Glen Blvd. in Los Angeles toward the end of his life. I can't remember the exact address anymore, but I do remember sitting in my car, trying to summon the courage to knock at the door and ask if he could give me some advice about my writing. The world was smaller then, and it felt less complicated though I'm sure it wasn't actually so. Thankfully, I never did manage the chutzpah to knock. Why am I thinking about distant memories which seem to have no relevance to my present situation? Especially those dreams of a twenty-six-year-old who wanted nothing more than to abandon the well-reasoned life, move to Paris, write pages upon pages of poetry, get lost in the Latin Quarter, devour the daring lives of Jean Rhys, Djuna Barnes, Colette, Henry Miller and Larry Durrell without the slightest thought of money or dentists or taxes or anything else remotely practical. Maybe I'm thinking about her because she once attempted at bravery.

It's been a month of tears for all of us at The Cross Border House, itself at a crossroads. The property we lease is being sold. We are closing our doors on July 1, 2023, unless we can find another place to live and continue our work. The residents here have been offered an opportunity to stay at their own expense, and some will do this. Others might be in a better position to find accommodation in the neighbouring town. But there are still those who don't have enough money to stay or to relocate without additional help, so of course this is our main concern.

If the Foundation is not able to secure a property, then we will divest the remaining funds at the end of June and do the best we can to help those who have no place to go figure out a solution.

This was not the war any of us expected.

On top of all this, the whole house is suffering from colds and flu, stomach viruses and now a chicken pox outbreak as of Friday night. I'd welcome the spring in my thoughts if it weren't for fear of stronger offensives, more deadly ones, more tanks, more missile strikes.

I cry without warning. The tears overcome me and before I know it, I must excuse myself. There is a code of decorum here among us and it's unspoken. We don't usually cry at the table. Tears well up; the eyes are watery but rarely does a drop fall. If that is about to happen, we depart. Yesterday I woke up hopeful, but by noon was in the car sobbing uncontrollably.

Yevgenia's husband, who came to see us over Christmas, Jana's daddy, is in the military. He was on the road this week with three other soldiers. He stopped the car so he could get out to smoke. The moment he was clear of the car, a missile hit the car and killed the three comrades left inside.

During this last offensive, Luba's daughter Marina and her husband, also in the military, have lost many, and yet they still stand. Luba is Stepan's grandmother. They live in Room Nine.

Across the hall is Oksana and her daughter Varvara, who decided to return to Ukraine yesterday despite the dangers; she was homesick and could never find her way here. Jordan packed her off with a goodly sum of travel money and the foundation bought her a sketchbook, a box of pencils and a soft toy. More tears shed as she drove away.

It takes the hard shell of steel to get through these days with a smile. Last week I started a diary entry I didn't finish:

'Igir bursts forth from the school bus very hungry. His mother can hardly contain him at the table as she quickly runs through to the kitchen to prepare his plate. He's not crying or demanding, just hungry. He's happy. He's full of energy and if he could tell you, I'm sure he would tell you what a wonderful day he had. I. has special needs. I don't know what they are but quite frankly that's not what's important. What is important though is to know that when he first came, he didn't smile much nor did he engage with anyone, but now I get the biggest hugs from him. So does Paul.

He makes eye contact. He's in school and playing and has a consistent and predictable routine.

'The children who were killed in the apartment building in Dnipro had lives too. They were maliciously murdered. Not by a stray missile, but by an intended one. A very powerful one.

'When you strip the uniform off a murderer, does he bear a soul? Is there a man or woman beneath this mask? Whoever those were who participated in this last missile strike didn't know the names of the children in that building in Dnipro. It could have been Igir coming home from school, hungry and happy and passing out hugs with his generous heart.

'It could have been Natalia who comes home sometimes not so happy and cranky until she gets her lunch but soon brightens and can always be counted on for a big hug.

It could have been any of the children here at The Cross Border House.

Bogdan. Paulina. Margo. Matvey. Olesya. Misha. Danilo. Volva. Jana. Swietek. Igir.

They have names and birthdays and stuffed toys and games they like to play. They are silly and mischievous, unreasonable and adorable. They are the children who deserve a chance to tell their story. They deserve to live. They all deserve to live their lives. Those who conspired to drop that bomb on the apartment building in Dnipro have not been denied their lives, and if they have children, nor have their children. Each of these murderers has a name.'

The work we are doing is essential. Grounding lives in continuity and a sense of daily certainty, allowing space for the psychological well-being of all, creating an environment of optimism and hope is and has been invaluable to each resident in this house.

My brother fought in the Vietnam War. He could tell you what war is like, but he doesn't talk about it and his family doesn't press. I don't think you're ever the same again. I am not in Ukraine, but the psyche of the house is there. Last night I dreamed I was on a bus going in and out of the country, crossing the border, picking up more people and bringing them here to safety. I know I will never be the same again.

I don't think it's always about acceptance. In fact, I think it's about resistance and resilience.

Gala, Jordan's fiancée, asked me to wait where I stood a few days ago. She went to her room and returned with the most beautiful painting. A painting? She felt like painting? Her brother is in the reserve military in Kyiv. She painted? Yes, she painted a lovely piece of art. One must resist. It's our only hope. We are doomed if we accept this war as "just the way it is."

This morning we woke to sunshine. It didn't last but it did improve my mood somewhat. We must at least try to resist the temptation to darkness even when the sun vanishes. It will come out again. It always does.

Meanwhile, the residents, Paul and I are all preparing to meet our future in the spirit of resilience and hope, in whatever form that takes. We must make art. We must be creative.

The residents in this house are among 103 other million displaced persons, according to the UNHCR, forcibly displaced by persecution, conflict, violence, human rights violations and events which seriously disturb public order.

I will never be the same again because my worldview has forever been impacted by the reality that there are those left homeless because of acts of war so egregious, so foolish, and so without merit, worth or reason and that these very demonstrations of stupidity disrupt generations to come which in turn will affect each and every one of us in some way or other throughout the course of time.

We do not need to know them personally to know that they have a name and a story. And the best we can do is to not demonize them but to open ourselves to their story, if lucky enough to come that close.

My husband's favourite uncle, Jan Rostworowski, was in the Polish army during WWII, stationed in St. Andrews, Scotland, when he received news that Paul's grandmother had died at the age of 42 in Wójcza. Wójcza is only about 20 minutes from here, the childhood home of Paul's mother. He wrote about what had been taken from him on the day the Nazis marched into Poland, followed not long after by the Russians.

> I run to greet the house, in every room
> A different story lurks, different echoes of
> well known melodies, of changing moods.
> The dining room is brown, a long table of walnut
> With sturdy curved legs.
> The sheen of the tabletop smiles back at us,
> With the smell of coffee and fresh bread.
> Breakfast
> a bouquet of dahlias in their silver basket
> Creates a splash of colour against the tabletop.
> By the wall richly carved sideboards, cupboards,
> stools. It appears
> Our mother, in her youth, drew the designs
> For the carvings. They both frighten and delight
> us children.
> Each head, column, side is carved in rich
> baroque. ...

A typical Polish country drawing room
Pastel coloured, straight out of 'Warszawianka'
You can still hear the musical notes quivering
in the lace curtains.
(Excerpt from "The Letter," Jan Rostworowski)

Were the deaths of approximately 70-85 million people and the loss of home, story, table and sweet memory worth WWII? What do we have to show? And now, more war. More disruption, more death.

You are the world as Krishnamurti said. You have to change before you can expect the world to change.

Knock, knock, Mr. Miller. Thank you for living in Big Sur for eighteen years with hardly enough money for much of anything but a crust of bread to feed you and your family. Despite what one might think of your work, or whatever they call you, painter, writer, raconteur or libertine, you made art your priority. You pursued the path of resistance. You resisted the status quo, the mundane, the banal. Your children tell us in interviews and newspaper articles that you told stories, every night. Made up ones. And you always had a glass of wine with dinner. The shop owner at the bottom of the hill accepted your drawings in exchange for supplies. You slipped away onto a high mountain cove and lived a peaceful life caring for your wife and two children. You lived your truth. You made art without the expectation of acknowledgment. You lived your life without interference. I stopped by today to say that your courage inspires me to live my truth, my life; especially when no one is watching.

February 15, 2023
Day 357

Since the last diary entry, there have been some developments that could be a game changer for The Cross Border House beyond July 1st.

While nothing is confirmed, there are some emerging prospects that look encouraging.

The Cross Border House applied for a sizeable EU grant which would provide a percentage of our annual financial needs over the next two years, putting us in a good position to actively fundraise for the rest.

The grant proposal will be assessed on a point criteria system, of which we believe we qualify in each category. This does not mean we will be awarded the grant; we simply feel we have a competitive edge. We will know by mid-March if we make the first pass.

I'm going back to my hometown in Houston, Texas, to put together a fundraiser with my family and some old friends who want to help me host an event highlighting the work of the foundation.

Another long-time friend of mine has made contact with all the high-profile media outlets in Houston and some have expressed the request for coverage. The idea is to overlap schedules so The Cross Border House can host a fundraising event with guaranteed media coverage. (*As I prepare to post this diary, KHOU-TV has contacted me for an interview.*)

Lastly, there is a former neighbour of mine who has offered to help us pitch our story to an international media giant, which, if successful, would generate another source of funds.

Our combined efforts have viable potential, enough to secure the core support we need to continue the project for another year. But we will not know for another two months. By mid-April we should know one way or another.

Marina, Stepan's mother and a Ukrainian soldier, came to our room to say goodbye today. She's returning to the front. Nothing ever prepares one to hear the stories firsthand. She said she spends many nights lying awake asking herself how is it that ordinary human beings can be so cruel. She was telling us about what's happening at the border of occupied Ukraine. It sounded like a scene out of *Schindler's List*. She watched a group of Ukrainian POW's reduced to emaciation. They were clearly starved. Then she watched the Russians shoot them all. She had also seen people in the town go out on errands and get shot at random if they encountered a soldier.

I have to at least try. I can't just say, "Oh well, not my war." I can't. So I will fight, tooth and nail, to improve our situation so that we can meet the rent required and carry on providing a safe place for the women and children here to ultimately be able to care for themselves.

According to Hannah Arendt, it's not so much about what one thinks but about what they don't think; in other words, the absence of thought which leads to what she called the "banality of evil."

How could such a nondescript, insipid character like Adolf Eichmann, a bureaucrat, dull as ditch water, rise to such power and commit the unspeakable crimes he did? Was it only because he wanted to acquire this level of status that he was able to justify the murder of millions of Jews without remorse? Or did he consciously, systematically set out to do this? He did keep saying at his trial that he was only following orders and would do it again if commanded. I don't know how he was able to do this, but what I do know is that his ability to discern what is moral and ethical against what is not was clearly within the realm of what Arendt would describe as the absence of thought.

One must draw a line in the sand and stand up in the face of adversity, ridicule, and any other dismissive action and make clear what is wrong. This war is wrong, and the women and the children forced into migration are vulnerable so long as they are without the full support they need. One cannot rationalize it for another person's convenience. If one cannot plainly, in each and every situation, stand by what is right, support a higher moral and ethical standard, then we all stand to succumb to the banality of evil.

June 17, 2023
Day 478

An Open Letter to:
Our generous donors from around the world
The Mima and John Fund at Greater Horizons
Marla, Dan and Carly Hodes in California
The Jung Centre/Sean Fitzpatrick/Houston,
Texas
Gabriella Nissen and Quinn Harris
David Lorimer
Melanie Robbins and Betsy Michau
The Poole Family
Denys and Sheelagh Reades
Karen Colenbrander
Basia Rostworowska

Dear All,

As we bring to a close our activities here in Sichów Duży, we want to thank everyone for their prayers, donations, kind thoughts, unwavering interest, and their willingness to share our story with others. We want to thank Stefan Dunin-Wąsowicz for sharing his property with us since the start of the war. It would have been impossible to have hosted so many without the space we were granted.

Our activities will begin anew, north of here about an hour from the German border. While we will not be hosting Ukrainians at Sichów, we will continue to apportion the monies we have to resettle the residents in independent housing. Our heartfelt thanks go to John Kulle for financing the Greater Horizons Grant that will help resettle families. We will provide periodic updates on The Cross Border House website.

Marina and her two boys left yesterday, bound for their new "now home" in the neighbouring town of Połaniec. (Her sister, Oksana, who is also a resident here, will join her soon.). They have a spacious, two-bedroom ground floor apartment with a small terrace and a community garden at the back. What makes it even more comfortable for them is knowing that the landlord has kindly welcomed them. There is a great peace when one feels safe in a new "now home". Most landlords across Poland do not rent to Ukrainians and I suppose one could argue endlessly over why, but I'm too tired to engage in such debates. That remains that not all are welcome. Such is the fallout from war and the unconscionable displacement of the vulnerable.

Nadia and her two children are moving tomorrow to another family property: Kurozweki Palace. The apartment made available to her is directly across the street from the school for children with special needs where her son is a student.

The Pechenizki's are moving to Krakow on June 21st. Masha has been accepted to the Jagiellonian University. She is a bright and disciplined girl who, at the age of 16, worked every day, studying into the night, tirelessly completing applications and documents until finally the day came when someone said, "Yes, we will take you." I'm sure there were times when she felt defeated, but I never saw it. A positive, can-do, try-harder attitude has visibly manifested in her.

The younger sister, Olesya, will take the entrance exam at the Ignacy Jan Paderewski Music School on Tuesday. This public school has a well-regarded music programme and is just around the corner from the family apartment.

Olesya was recently awarded 2nd place in all of Ukraine in the junior division of chess – ages up to 16. This eight-year-old will have the chance to continue developing her skills in Krakow.

Our nephew, Jordan Poole, who volunteered his time, his love and his skill as a first responder at The Cross Border House, has gone back to Texas. He came to us in March 2022, at the beginning of the war. There wasn't anything he couldn't repair, from bicycles to washing machines. He was our Friday night cook. He was our taxi driver and the one who kept his wits about him when Paul and I were in a state of falling apart. He worked with Gala on art activities with the children and could wrap a present like a pro. Thank you, Jordan. We miss you!

Katya and her family are now working in Staszow, and as soon as her son, Bogdan, is finished with school, they will move into their apartment in town.

We are still looking for a place for Yuliia Cheban and her three but are confident we will find something soon.

Luba and Stepan are going back to Ukraine, as are Oksana and her mother, Iryna. Oksana said that in Kharkiv it's not so dangerous at the moment, though there are definite food shortages, and if it gets too bad, they will go to the shelters in Kyiv.

Yevgenia and Yuliia and their two little ones, Jana and Svetik, are coming with us to Poznan. They simply have no one except some family in Zaporizhzhia, and Yevgenia's husband is in the war so his whereabouts are unpredictable and always changing. We have a short-term lease for them in an apartment in Poznan while we look for a permanent solution.

The Litoshko family will move to Kielce. Our cousin Stefan is working on temporary housing for them there.

Oksana and her children will also relocate in Kielce, close to the hospital.

This will be my last war diary from Sichów. I wanted to write something profound, something of philosophic interest, but honestly, I'm exhausted. What I can say with undisputed clarity, exhaustion aside, is how grateful I am to everyone who stood by us every step of the way: **Our Donors**, each and every one.

GRACIOUS THANKS:

To John Kulle and Greater Horizons for a generous grant. This grant is the reason we are able to resettle every resident in the house, helping them launch an autonomous, independent life in their own apartments near to their workplace and near to schools.

Thank you to MARLA and DAN HODES who offered to host a benefit in California and to their friends who came through with $10,000 which has served to support us up to July 1st.

Great thanks to Melanie and Betsy for coming all the way from America with suitcases full of donations and making pizzas for the children. We will never forget you.

Thank you to HOUSTON, my hometown where FAMILY and friends and volunteers gathered together at THE JUNG CENTRE which so graciously opened their doors to host our event. A special thanks to Sean Fitzpatrick, Director, for making that happen and to Gabriella Nissen and Quinn Harris who said, 'Yes, we will help.'

A special recognition to the actors: Sheryl Croix, Michelle Britton, Fritz Dickmann, Susan Blair, Magdalen

Vaughn, Pamela Vogel, Jim Lawrence, Roxanne Claire, and Paige Moore who gave generously their time and professionalism.

Josh Poole and Xachary Blunt for supervising the audio visual and tech set up. Thanks to photographer Jeff McMorrough for donating his time and talent, gifting TCBH with great pictures of the event.

Heartfelt thanks to Andrei Sinclair, who joined us from London last year to play with the children inside and out, creating art from nature and story.

Thank you to Alan Schnitger and Ben Tuma of Iron Archelon for all of their support in the design and management of the beautiful Cross Border House website.

Volunteers in Poland: Jordan Poole, Andrii Pechenizkyi, Yulia Pechenizka, Maria Pechenizka-Tkachova, Olesya Pechenizka-Tkachova, Gala Pechenizka.

All the Ukrainian Residents at The Cross Border House.

Thank you to my dear cousin Basia Rostworoska for calling every week, for visiting several times, for reading and recording every single war diary on Morley College Radio and in her way, assuring that no one she knew would forget about us.

Thank you, David Lorimer, for donating the proceeds to your inspiring book of poetry: *Better Light A Candle.*

Thank you to our daughter's family, Denys and Sheelagh Reades, along with their Canadian prayer groups who have been consistently remembering us in prayer since February 2022. The power of this goodwill is tangible. We are grateful. Thanks especially to Karen Colenbrander.

Unfortunately, I was never able to realise my dream of creating a permanent place, a permanent centre for those fleeing from war, a dream which is still wholly misunderstood by most, so allow me to set the record straight here from a letter printed in the *Guardian* on May 23, 2023. What the Georgian government has done to aid its refugee population is exactly the solution I had hoped for here.

> Regarding the letter on how the government's housing plan will put refugees' lives at risk: I am the chair of trustees of the charity Refugees Welcome, Cheshire East. Earlier this month, I visited the Tserovani refugee settlement in Georgia. The settlement of about 2,000 homes was built in 2008 to house refugees from South Ossetia made homeless by the conflict between the Russian Federation and Georgia. It took around three months to build the small but sound houses for the victims.
>
> People have extended the homes and created gardens around them. Transport infrastructure is part of the plan so that people can go to work in nearby towns. *What's important is that they feel safe.*
>
> Jobs have been created in the settlement, such as a social enterprise jewellery workshop, which we were fortunate enough to attend. *Desperate people have dignity and are able to contribute to the economy of their new arena.*
>
> What a shame it is that our government is unable to understand and embrace the needs of refugees who come to the UK. *How wonderful it would be if suitable homes for refugees and other displaced people could be built, rather than endless estates of four-bedroom houses.*

Nicky Campbell
Macclesfield, Cheshire

I might add, Nicky Campbell, that the U.K. is not the only country that does not understand, nor does its citizens. Not in the least.

In another article from the *Guardian* printed on June 6, 2023, titled: "How We Survive. "At 12, I was in Auschwitz. My parents and seven siblings were murdered. Here is how I built a life."

Ivor Perl is the survivor, and the article begins with a question; a question he asks the journalist.

"How much has it helped in the 80 years, us talking?"

By "us", he means fellow survivors of the Holocaust who have testified to the horrors they witnessed. He wants to know if all the talks at schools, all the media interviews, have achieved anything. "Can you tell me?" I ask him to answer his own question.

"I think: nothing." He urges me to "look around the world" – at Ukraine, at Sudan, at China's treatment of the Uyghur Muslims. "So I would like to know, is there anything the world has learned from us?

Absolutely nothing.

Amber Poole Kieniewicz
June 8, 2023
Sichów Duży, Poland

The Bewilderment of
Being of a War Refugee

~

A Fundraising Talk, Houston, 2023

There are seven different types of refugees, within each classification a life-threatening reason to leave one's homeland. Hunger, persecution, physical violence, those without documentation, otherwise known as stateless, but in this case, war.

Lawrence Hillman, James Hillman's son, once told me that his father said to him: 'When you have a problem, make it really big so you can see it.'

So I came back to Texas, my home state, where everything is really big, to look at this problem, to see if we can't see it together.

What does it feel like to be a war refugee?

All that was once relegated to the news or to another corner of the world, or to those things that happened to someone else is suddenly prominent in the life of a war refugee. The threat of poverty, homelessness, forced migration, human trafficking, exploitation, isolation and loneliness.

Add to this, uncertainty, fear and unfavourable public perception.

How do we get it wrong when we open the doors to a large stadium or church banquet hall, set up cots and provide boxed meals? With all of our best intentions, how do we get it wrong, how do we get it right? We get it wrong because we don't finish the work. In the case of the Ukrainians fleeing war, we get it wrong because we don't understand the psychology of what has just happened to 8 million people.

We get it right, because at least we try. But we're going to have to try harder. When 2.5 million people cross your border looking for their new livelihood, it's best not to ignore their presence.

On February 28, 2022, the bus loads of Ukrainian refugees started arriving to Sichów, my home in Poland. There was a ground swell of enthusiasm in the country. There were volunteers at train stations, there were kiosks set up at border towns to assist young mothers and their children, their senior family members, with shelter options, care packages, and government officials assuring their safety here, every hand stretched out, every door flew open to welcome these road worn, traumatised exiles, until one by one, the doors started closing, the enthusiasm waning, the subsidies drying up, as indifference emerged within the public perception.

How do we get it wrong? How do we get it right?

By April, 2022, we had forty refugees living with us. These core forty are still with us today.

Here is our story.

Ten days before Russia invaded Ukraine, Paul and I were invited to a Valentine's Day dinner. Our nephew sent a driver for us so we could both enjoy the champagne and festivities. We were in a lively conversation with guests at the table about what our programs for 2022 looked like. For the past seven years, Paul and I had run an educational centre offering courses in spiritual growth, inter-faith workshops, theatre classes taught in English, and a variety of outdoor summer activities for children.

It was during this conversation that someone asked Paul what he would do if there was war. Would he agree to taking in refugees? That close to the invasion, Paul was certain there would be war and said, "I can't not receive them. When the first bus arrives, I will open the doors." I didn't believe there would be such an invasion, myself. The idea that such a thing could happen was beyond my imagination. To ask that I visualise a bus carrying victims of war showing up at my door seemed so surreal to me that I dismissed the whole notion of it.

Still, our dreams were warning us. And we take dreams very seriously.

On February 28, 2022, the buses did arrive.

Nothing in my history of living has ever prepared me for the fourteen months I've spent in a community among war refugees.

On March 8, 2022 I started to keep a war diary. I've been faithful to this diary until recently when I had to prepare for my trip to America. It's a chronicle of my observations, of happenings in the house, of stories that come to us from Ukraine, in general, a documentation of events.

The first week we spent together as a community, we called a meeting. In that welcome speech I said.

"We consider you as our guests and we are here to serve you. As a woman and a mother, I am particularly passionate about your comfort and your well-being. In particular about your specific needs.

I am also very aware of the need for you to maintain your own sense of dignity, way of living and routine, as best as is possible under the circumstances. Paul and I are here to help you with that.

Finally, it is of great importance to me, that for as long as you are here, you feel the freedom of protection and safety for yourselves and for your children.

We are a community now, even if only for a little while or a long while. Being in a community means that every voice is important. Please do not hesitate to ask for what you need and to share your feelings if you so desire."

The sentiment in this opening speech is a cornerstone upon which we base our decisions at The Cross Border House. I think the website says it best: The Cross Border House is a sanctuary for the Ukrainian residents in which they can reclaim their sense of human dignity, hope and optimism. This is the goal.

Basic provisions are not enough to create a facility offering a high standard of holistic care. How do we get it right? How do we get it wrong?

What is most important is to know what you're holding in your arms. What have you said yes to, and to what level of commitment have you said yes? Who are these strangers among you who now live in your kitchen, in your living room, your dining room, your study, your outdoors, who sit at your table, who are there when you wake up and there when you go to bed. Strangers all to each other. One way to look at it is to visualise yourself on a subway. Visualise yourself stepping onto the train.

Say, forty people in one car and that car freezes in time and space and each of you make your way, one with the other. You have lost everything. You have lost your home, your belongings, your pets, your country, your dreams, and in some cases, family members and friends. Nothing will ever be the same again.

I can tell you that it's both one of the most rewarding and most surprising occurrences in my life. If anyone here is interested in fast-track shadow work, come to The Cross Border House for a year or two; you'll graduate with honours.

On May 28, 2022, Day 94 of the War, I wrote in my diary:

Let me start with a short anecdote. When I worked at the Jung Centre in Houston, Jim Hollis was the director, my boss. For those of you who don't know Jim's work, I strongly encourage you to look him up and order any of his books, all of his books. You can't go wrong.

One day when I showed up for work in a bad mood much like "Alexander and the Terrible, Horrible No Good Very Bad Day", Alexander who wants to move to Australia, I arrived to work in this state. In fact, I think I must have said something to that effect that I'd like to move to Australia. And Jim, in his infinite wisdom, in his dry response, said, "Just remember, wherever you go you take yourself with you."

What I want to share today has been on my mind for a while and I'd like to set the record straight. I get the distinct impression that there are those who read these diaries who think that Sichów is a kind of Arcadia. Some kind of pastoral fairyland where we all get along and work together in this harmonious bubble without discord. Well it's not.

Nothing could be further from the truth.

As we have become more familiar with each other, it's nothing that we crowd shoulder to shoulder at the stove, a little push to ensure our portion is properly dished out and maybe some of another's onto our plate. It's nothing to us now to carve out our personal space at the tea kettle for a cup of coffee, even it that means overlapping with your neighbour also waiting for the water to boil or take the last slice of cake for instance or lay siege to the baskets of strawberries as they're delivered to the back door.

Not everyone who showed up that day in February came with charity in their hearts or a sense of fair play and for those who were self-centred before the war, well...they're still self-centred as the war rages on and will be, likely, at its end. This is how we are. You can't take the human out of humans.

But when you're motivated by something greater than yourself, something outside of yourself that throughout the years has encouraged an inner journey to self-discovery, to some sense of gnosis, then you are able to see with a greater discernment.

End of Diary Entry.

Why does The Cross Border House work so well? It's a high functioning shelter in spite of us humans who live there. Or should I say because of us humans who live there. Seriously though, how is it that we are able, with all of our psychological nuances and colliding personalities, live in such close quarters and not clear out? I'm sure there isn't a day that goes by that one or another want to bolt, but in spite of this intermittent impulse, we stay. Why?

To adequately provide each resident the opportunity for renewed clarity, it is imperative to create an atmosphere of complete acceptance. When there is access to free time and to both private and communal space, the resident can begin to consider a way forward in their life.

This means that each individual must be consciously considered, with all of his or her moving parts, front and centre above any other agenda.

Wow. What does that mean?

One of the ways we get it wrong is to think that food and shelter are enough. In some places, such as Zervou Refugee Camp on the island of Samos, asylum seekers have been living like animals for the past two years, surviving on a sub-nutritious diet, living in either tents or flat packs, without proper sanitation or even consistent healthcare with only one medic for the 3,500 residents.

In the UK and Poland alike, hotels are renting out rooms to Ukrainians, charging for basic meals but with no other assistance such as the offering of intermediary services to understand job opportunities, accommodation options and legal rights. Most are languishing in this state until the war is over so they can go home. Unfortunately, for many, returning home is not an option which makes the life of the war refugees that much harder.

How do we get it wrong?

We're missing the point. We're paying millions of dollars, five to ten to be exact, to create these monstrous camps with minimal staffing, relying only on whatever foreign, humanitarian aid can mitigate as a result.

How do we get it right?

Small numbers, multiple shelters. Earmark a portion of those millions and distribute among the few, create a healthy, sustainable living system, encourage autonomy through individual potential, with an agenda of integration.

The closer one can stay to his or her own place of origin, of course, the easier it is to assimilate. In this sense, the Ukrainians have an advantage to those coming from Africa or the Middle East looking to settle in Europe because the fluid borders in Eastern Europe have been shape shifting for thousands of years. Ukrainians are essentially first cousins to the Poles, making communication and cultural identities easier to blend through language, cuisine and humour.

The Cross Border House is two hours from the Ukrainian border. Not all are so fortunate as to find shelter this close to their roots.

On June 18, 2022, Day 115, I wrote:

What does it mean to be an exile? I frequently ask myself this question.

When my husband's parents, Rose and Henry Kieniewicz, crossed into Scotland with nothing but the clothes on their backs and the shoes in which they stood, they knew no one except other exiles from a defunct Polish army. The living conditions for this young couple were deeply dissatisfying. Rose gave birth to her daughter, Theresa, shortly after they arrived and had trouble keeping her quiet. Imagine that. The prickly, old landlady wasn't amused. To say the least, she placed unrealistic demands on them to keep a newborn baby quiet.

So when Rose and Henry finally settled in an old stone cottage provided for them by the Earl of Scone Palace, it opened up like a castle for Rose. With no indoor plumbing and no heat other than that of a paraffin stove, she recounts her sense of jubilation that she now had her own home. Her privacy was once again restored. Her babies could fit and cry in freedom.

I do encounter some visitors to Sichów who are surprised by the high functioning level of activity and often sense in their surprise a measure of subtle reproach.

I ask the question. Why should people, classified as refugees, be so fortunate as to have access to an art studio in which to paint, draw or craft or a sewing machine endowed with good quality fabrics and threads on which to make clothes or tablecloths? Isn't this a luxury reserved only for those in a settled political situation?

Why should these refugees be treated to soft fruits such as strawberries, served with cream and sugar when they are in a position of charity? Are not these amenities reserved only for those who work hard, pay taxes, those of whom are in a stable and established circumstance, those who can afford such things? Is it even our ethical responsibility to allow a foreigner such a delicacy; or is it good enough to simply supply bread, water, cheese, porridge and a bed? Does it not provoke resentment from the local population who see this level of charity when they themselves are struggling economically? Should not the foreigner instead accept their station in a reduced class, an uninvited guest, and submit to a lower wage earning status of field and housework?

Personally, I don't find these questions complicated because I literally believe that all the residents living here today are equal to me and I to them. Nothing separates us but history, place and personal interests. All the same I can understand the bitterness in these small Polish villages hamstrung by decades of communist oppression.

Quoting Rose: "If anyone told me that by the time I was twenty-five I'd be living in Scotland, I would have said they were from the moon."

The philosophy behind The Cross Border House model of sheltering and rebuilding depends on a few key points. The defining of the words charity, dignity, and the psychology of the individual are integral to the way Paul and I conduct ourselves and the decisions we make.

The art studio is here to maintain dignity. So is the sewing centre. Some have already lost their homes, some fear they will be next but all share in the loss of a country, at least for the moment. All are out of place. All are victims of war.

Unfortunately, we live in a world now of collective psychosis and there are some very precious children here who should be fiercely protected. One of the ways we protect is to provide. Sichów is a child's garden of verse and play. In the art studio are drawing and painting classes and in the library room upstairs are books, puzzles, games and toys. (And as I've said before, if you're lucky enough to be here on Tuesdays and Fridays you can listen in on Paul giving Olesya a recorder lesson. Magic.) The healthy psychology of a community is based on the health of the individual. If the residents here are at moderate peace and if Sichów can lessen their anxieties, then we stand a good chance at maintaining a community in balance.

When the children first came to Sichów, they were so quiet. They burrowed into their mothers side, hardly ever making eye contact. Certainly never arguing about what was on the plate in front of them. In those beginning days, it was more like living in a religious order than a shelter. I thought to myself that the Ukrainians must possess the great secret to raising such well behaved children. Yet at the same time, I thought it wasn't normal for children to be so composed.

How do we get it right, how do we get it wrong?

We get it wrong when a child cannot express himself without fear of being relocated. In the case of children fleeing war, they are first removed to underground city shelters amounting to a sense of confusion. Then the trauma of missile strikes and air raid sirens roaring overhead create a feeling of powerlessness. Later, they're tossed headlong into the perplexity of a nomadic way of life, compounding further the uneasiness and complications of their circumstances. Travelling on foot roads unfamiliar to them, often without enough food or a place to sleep.

It didn't take long after sheltering at Sichów that things changed.

If I have painted a picture of the library where they at first gathered, playing quietly and politely, with puzzles and games and cooperatively building lego together, nothing now could be further from the truth. We need about four official referees and an emergency medical team to cover that area.

They're doing what they're supposed to be doing. They're being children. In fact, most mischievous ones.

An example.

When the mandarins were at their sweetest last summer and reasonably priced, I bought them by the box load. Our orders come in on Monday, Wednesday and Friday. We should have been covered. As the days passed, I was surprised that we were noticeably running low, if not completely out of oranges. Of course, I immediately blamed this shortage on my nemesis, but then I blame her for everything – even things that happened before I met her. Living together with strangers is not always easy, but it is entertaining and it does offer a glimpse into a gigantic mirror, if willing to look.

I went back and checked my invoices and thought that the amount I was ordering should have been enough to carry us through from order to order and this went on for a couple of weeks until one day, Artful Dodger ran past the kitchen door at breakneck speed. He didn't see me standing there. He was carrying a grocery bag as big as he was. And there, in plain sight, shovelling mandarins into the bag. And then whistling for his gang who came running in from the other end of the corridor with bags of equal size and they too started helping themselves. I absolutely shrieked. "Damned delinquents. What are you doing stealing all the oranges? Get out of here. Out out out." The gang members dropped their bags and ran off. But not the Dodger. Nope. He stared me down, strategically backing away, ever so tightly clutching that bag of fruit. He wasn't about to let go of his steal. The child standing in front of me could have easily been my own, his friends and cousins. Zach, Josh, Jordan. Healthy, playful, naughty boys.

The children at the Cross Border House are not home free by any means, but at least they're in a place where they have the good fortune to express themselves without fear of eviction.

My husband's family never truly integrated into the British culture. This is not to say they didn't have a good life there, only to say that it's unnatural to be aborted from ones culture of origin by force. Everything familiar is left behind.

No war is any different from any other war in this sense. All war produces this displacement of its citizens. All wars leave them homeless and vulnerable.

I propose to use the word support rather than charity. To partner, even better. Never lose sight of the dignity in another regardless of how you feel about them. This is not easy because they may not be demonstrating the same toward you, themselves or others. But because we live in a structured environment I believe we can practice this level of respect toward each other with a bit less difficulty.

We do not live lavishly, we live creatively. We must live creatively if we are to maintain psychological health.

End of Diary Entry for Day 115 of a war still perpetrating genocide.

One of my favourite Ingmar Bergman films is one called, *Shame*. Speaking in an interview from 1968, he says: "It just turned out that way. I felt that these people before this great war broke loose all around them, should end up in some place, where time had stopped ... with all these wars in which two great powers collide...you can't help but identify with the third parties caught in the middle. I suppose that's the fear we all carry inside."

In his irrefutable genius, he was able to capture on camera man's utmost vulnerability. *Shame*. It's not what I expected. But when living in a community of war refugees for over a period of time and if you're compassionately observing, shame is the burden carried by all. Sitting across the table from you is a man in his early seventies who had a home and a routine, something to show you when you came to visit. Something he was proud to show you. A table to lay, a bed for you to sleep in, a chair by the fire. Now he sits in your home, with nothing, and must accept your charity.

Every day is an opportunity for meditation at The Cross Border House. Everyday forces you to look a little bit deeper. At least it is for me and I know it is as well for Paul and true for Jordan Poole, my nephew who came to help out in March, 2022 who is still with us. And maybe for others this is also true but considering the language barrier I wouldn't really know.

In order to make our lives work together, frozen in time such as we are, the ethos of our care must be to tread lightly and lovingly, honouring the dignity in each, even and especially during those moments of conflict and misunderstanding. One of the ways we do this is to help the residents understand that it isn't us paying for the food, but the Foundation which has been generously funded by donors from around the world.

In that spirit, The Cross Border House Team was able to assess what was needed for the psychological well-being of each.

We got it right.

Still, it's essential that you know, living in a shelter is not natural. No matter how much care is provided. Living in a shelter is like being in prison for a crime you didn't commit. Strawberries and cream and cake make it a little easier but the goal is always, always to restore one to his or her own previous level of independence and routine.

EPILOGUE

A Love Story

~

Can a love story root in the midst of war, in a foreign country, in two languages, each unknown to the other, cultures as dissimilar – one to the other – as unrecognisable as a fish is to the fowl, can love bloom in the shadows of hatred, bloodshed, tears and loss? Yes. It can. And it did. At the Cross Border House, a love story so strong and tender that it flourishes to this day.

In March, 2022, my nephew, Jordan Poole came to Poland. He was fed-up with his job. He was lonely, looking for something, but what and where and how to realize such, he hadn't a clue. That's when he decided to take a break from Houston and come to help us at the shelter. He thought that some time away from his routine, especially a sabbatical from a job he disliked would inspire him to draw again. (Jordan has studied art since high school; drawing is his preference and in my opinion, his great talent.)

His arrival at The Cross Border House couldn't have been better timed. We needed him to offload the everyday chores we bore, like grocery shopping, occasional cleaning, preparing rooms for incoming residents, driving and general maintenance. Ultimately, he became our confidant and moral support.

Gala Pechenizka arrived in the middle of the night, on a bus, running away from the bombardment of Kharkiv by an unprovoked Russian invasion. No one expected the war to last but just a few weeks.

The Ukrainian residents were emphatic about enrolling their children in school. Paul and I were much more concerned about their well-being and asked if they wouldn't as well consider psychological support for such a traumatic occurrence to which a searching gaze fixed their expressions in place and they politely declined.

When the weeks turned into months, Jordan had the great idea to create a work space for arts and crafts and related activities; a place for both the adults and the children. The Pechenizkyi's earned their living as artists before the war so Jordan and Gala got busy planning this space together. Jordan's idea was to restore as much integrity to the individual life of each resident, as before it had been aborted by war.

This idea turned out to be a real success story. We put on plays, developed after school activities, drawing and painting classes that even the local children enjoyed in participating.

It's impossible for me to say when the magic of love seeded as I am only a bystander. I did notice the two of them spending more and more time together in the gallery, their easels parked next to each other and long summer night walks with Gala's family and the dogs happily trailing alongside.

As the winter approached, Gala made breakfast for us every morning. Jordan was there to help. Often, she was crafting a new project to keep the children occupied. Jordan was there to help. There were the holidays and children's parties, which required costumes and cakes, and all of these were tended by their loving hands.

The shelter was a sacred place for all of us. Of course it couldn't last forever, and while you're in the midst of it, with all of its demands and challenges, it doesn't always feel sacred or like you'd even want it to last forever, but it was so, a sacred space for those who'd been cast out of place.

When it became clear that we would all have to move, Gala and Jordan made their plans. He would return to Houston and to the job he left behind, help to settle the family in Krakow so Masha, Gala's niece, could attend university and then wait for his beloved to join him. After the endurance of a five-month separation, Gala was cleared to enter the United States. Jordan returned to Krakow in early October to accompany his bride-to-be back to Texas.

Within a humanity that is rapidly destroying itself through massacre, hatred, and ignorance, I am here to report that there is still hope and that love does bud in the most unlikely places.

The Pechenizkyi's and the Pooles are now one family. From Texas to Ukraine, two diverse cultures, two different languages, two separate countries are now making one place together, connected for life.

As a postscript, I failed to mention that Jordan didn't speak a word of Ukrainian while Gala spoke only a limited amount of English.

I have known Jordan all of his life and what I admire most about this story is his resolve. His commitment to her and hers to him in a time when words like loyalty, trust, promise, responsibility, pledge, duty and obligation are old fashioned and easily replaced with the more self-indulgent, less constant ones like burdensome, bothersome, difficult, complicated, all things considered, inconvenient. Most people today would not have demonstrated the same fortitude as these two, to their great credit.

Relationships are not easy, but rewarding. Jordan and Gala give me hope that a world where courage will outweigh cowardice is still possible. It is the preservation of these traditional values that will perhaps influence the next generation to make a more principled choice about how they treat another human being.

Amber, Józef Mehoffer Gallery. In front of Portrait
of Paul's Great Uncle Karol Hubert Rostworowski,
Poland's National Playwright (1877-1938)

About the Author

Amber Poole is a long time student of Jungian
psychology and former Program Manager of the
Jung Centre Houston. She is a graduate of the
Edward Albee Advanced Playwriting Master's Class,

1998-2001, University of Houston School of Theatre and Dance. She is the Vice-President of the Sichowska Funadacja Edukacjna, an educational charity in Poland active since 2017.

Since the outbreak of the Ukrainian war, the Foundation has hosted over 70 refugees seeking food and shelter. Her work is exclusively dedicated to those displaced by war, famine, human rights violations and persecution.

She is a permanent resident of Poland, where she lives with her husband, Paul Kieniewicz.

Milton Keynes UK
Ingram Content Group UK Ltd.
UKHW010132270224
438425UK00002B/3